PERFECT
PRESERVES

PERFECT PRESERVES

how to make the best
jams and jellies ever

an essential guide to home
preserving with over 75
delicious step-by-step recipes
for sweet fruit conserves

MAGGIE MAYHEW

southwater

This edition is published by Southwater

Southwater Books is an imprint of Anness Publishing Ltd
Hermes House, 88–89 Blackfriars Road, London SE1 8HA
tel. 020 7401 2077; fax 020 7633 9499
www.southwaterbooks.com; www.annesspublishing.com

If you like the images in this book and would like to investigate using them for publishing, promotions or advertising,
please visit our website www.practicalpictures.com for more information.

UK agent: The Manning Partnership Ltd,
tel. 01225 478444; fax 01225 478440; sales@manning-partnership.co.uk
UK distributor: Grantham Book Services Ltd, tel. 01476 541080; fax 01476 541061; orders@gbs.tbs-ltd.co.uk
North American agent/distributor: National Book Network, tel. 301 459 3366; fax 301 429 5746; www.nbnbooks.com
Australian agent/distributor: Pan Macmillan Australia, tel. 1300 135 113; fax 1300 135 103; customer.service@macmillan.com.au
New Zealand agent/distributor: David Bateman Ltd,
tel. (09) 415 7664; fax (09) 415 8892

Publisher: Joanna Lorenz
Editorial Director: Judith Simons
Managing Editor: Linda Fraser
Project Editors: Susannah Blake and Jennifer Mussett
Production Controller: Claire Rae
Photographer: Craig Robertson
Home Economist: Sarah O'Brien
Stylist: Helen Trent

Previously published as part of a larger volume, *Preserves*.

ETHICAL TRADING POLICY
Because of our ongoing ecological investment programme, you, as our customer, can have the pleasure and reassurance of knowing
that a tree is being cultivated on your behalf to naturally replace the materials used to make the book you are holding. For further
information about this scheme, go to www.annesspublishing.com/trees

NOTES
Bracketed terms are intended for American readers. Medium (US large) eggs are used unless otherwise stated.
For all recipes, quantities are given in both metric and imperial measures and, where appropriate, measures are also given in
standard cups and spoons. Follow one set, but not a mixture, because they are not interchangeable.
Standard spoon and cup measures are level.
1 tsp = 5ml, 1 tbsp = 15ml, 1 cup = 250ml/8fl oz
Australian standard tablespoons are 20ml. Australian readers should use 3 tsp in place of 1 tbsp for measuring small quantities.
This book has been written with the reader's safety in mind, and the advice, information and instructions are intended to be clear and safe
to follow. However, cooking with boiling hot mixtures can be dangerous and there is a risk of burns if sufficient care is not taken. Neither the
author nor the publisher can accept any legal responsibility or liability for any errors or omissions made, or for accidents in the kitchen.

contents

INTRODUCTION

Preserving seasonal fruits as jams and jellies is one of the oldest of culinary arts. Once essential for basic survival, preserving is nowadays more often employed for the wealth of rich flavours it can bring to every meal or snack. It can be done in two ways: by heat sterilization, which destroys enzymes and bacteria, or by creating an environment where contaminants are unable to thrive – by drying or by adding sugar, salt, vinegar or alcohol.

AN AGE-OLD TECHNIQUE

Preserving was one of the earliest skills acquired by man, essential for survival during the cold, dark winter months when fresh food was scarce. Sun and wind were the first natural agents to be used: fruits and vegetables laid out in the hot sun or hung in the wind to dry were found to last longer than fresh produce and were lighter and easier to carry. In colder, damp climates, smoke and fire were used to hasten the drying process.

These discoveries meant that travelling to new territories became easier and new settlements were built where it was feasible for people to both grow and store food. It wasn't long before early man found that salt was a powerful dehydrator, far more consistent and reliable than the natural elements of sun and wind. The preservative properties of vinegar and alcohol were discovered around the same time, and people also realized that food could be flavoured at the same time that it was being preserved.

Surprisingly the use of sugar as a preservative wasn't discovered until many centuries later. Cane sugar, brought to Europe by Arab merchants in the 12th century, remained a scarce luxury in the Western world for 400 years. It wasn't until the 16th century, when it was introduced to Europe from the West Indies, that sugar became a sought-after ingredient. Soon the demand for it became so great that it encouraged the rise of colonialism and the slave trade. In the 18th century, beetroot (beet), which had always been enjoyed as a vegetable, began to be cultivated specifically for its sugar content. Eventually sugar became plentiful and cheap, and the liking for sweet preserves started to grow.

It was during the 19th century that preserving really came into its own and was considered to be a skilled craft adopted in most households. Many of the recipes we use today are based on those that first appeared in cookbooks during that era. Housewives took pride in filling capacious pantries with an array of bottles and jars of sweet preserves, jams, jellies and marmalades. Most of these were made during the summer and autumn when berries and fruits were fresh and plentiful. These were then enjoyed during the lean winter months to supplement the diet, which would otherwise have consisted mainly of salted meats and root vegetables.

In the 20th century, preserving became less fashionable. Many homes had less storage space and, as the range and use of commercially prepared foods and preserves increased, huge stocks of home-made preserves were no longer needed or desirable.

Left: Rich, fruity jams have been a traditional method for preserving fruit for many centuries.

Above: Placing fruits in flavoured syrups was one of the earliest ways that sugar was used for preserving.

Imported produce meant that many fruits were available all year round – soft fruits could be bought in the winter months and citrus fruits never disappeared from grocers' shelves. By the middle of the century, refrigerators could be found in most homes, followed by freezers in the 1960s and 70s, and during those decades freezing became the preferred way of preserving fruit and vegetables and the old-fashioned techniques became less popular.

PRESERVE-MAKING TODAY

Nowadays, the art of preserving is coming back into its own, not because food needs to be processed to make it keep for long periods but for reasons of quality and variety. Improved travel and communication have increased knowledge of preserves from around the world and more unusual varieties of

Right: Nowadays fruit-packed home-made jams and conserves have become culinary treats.

fruit and flavouring ingredients are now readily available. Many people prefer to make their own preserves instead of buying mass-produced products with artificial flavourings and colourings. The satisfaction that comes from being able to create a unique product – especially when you have grown or picked your own fruit – is also being rediscovered. In some parts of the world it has become a flourishing cottage industry, with villages and towns becoming renowned for the quality of jams and other preserves, often focusing on locally grown or gathered fruits. The ease with which jams and preserves can be made in the home with simple equipment and ingredients makes jam-making a practical and enjoyable occupation for many in rural and urban environments alike.

This book contains a comprehensive and detailed reference section showing how to make jams and other sweet preserves. All the main techniques are shown, including jam-, jelly- and marmalade-making; bottling fruits; candying; and drying. There is also a fabulous full-colour guide to the ingredients used for preserving – from seasonal fruits to flavourings and preservatives.

The stunning recipe collection includes a whole host of traditional and contemporary ideas that will prove to be an inspiration and pleasure to both the novice jam-maker and the experienced preserver.

SOFT FRUITS AND BERRIES

These delicate fruits are the epitome of summer and early autumn and can be made into wonderful jams and jellies. Despite their distinctive flavours and appearance, many are interchangeable in recipes. They can also be preserved in alcohol, but are less successful when bottled in syrup. Soft berries are most often used in jams and conserves, while currants and cranberries are particularly good made into jellies.

STRAWBERRIES

These fruits are one of the most popular berries for jam-making and have a wonderfully fragrant flavour. Choose medium-size berries with an intense fragrance as these will give the preserve a good fruity flavour. Look for just-ripe, firm, fresh berries and use them for jam-making as soon as possible after picking, as this is when the pectin content is highest. Rinse

Below: Strawberries are one of the most popular fruits for jam-making.

Right: Raspberries can be made into intensely flavoured jams, jellies and conserves.

them only if absolutely necessary, wiping with a cloth instead. If you do wash them, don't cut or hull them beforehand, or water will penetrate the fruit.

Tiny wild strawberries (*fraises de bois*), also known as alpine strawberries, have a pungent aroma and flavour and can be used whole in conserves.

THE RASPBERRY AND BLACKBERRY FAMILY

Technically, each berry is composed of multiple fruits as every tiny segment contains a hard seed. Jams made from these fruits have a high seed content, so they are often strained and made into seedless jams or jellies. The true raspberry is a bright crimson colour; yellow and white raspberries are also available and these have a deliciously delicate flavour, but they make less attractive preserves.

Related to the raspberry, blackberries are a wild fruit, native to Europe and the United States. They are now grown commercially to produce larger, juicier berries. Blackberries contain sufficient pectin to make intensely flavoured jellies, and go extremely well with apples. This classic combination originally came about because early ripening apples were scarce and wild blackberries could be used to make them go further.

Dewberries are closely related to the blackberry and are similar in appearance. Cloudberries, which grow in North America and Canada, are a bright orange-red colour; the Scandinavian (or Arctic) cloudberry, which also grows in Scotland, is a pinky yellow colour with an almost caramel flavour. Loganberries (a cross between the raspberry and the Pacific blackberry) look like elongated, very dark raspberries but have a juicier, fuller flavour. Tayberries are a similar hybrid and are large, conical and deep purple. Boysenberries are long, dark red berries with a sharp flavour. All these berries can be successfully preserved in the same way as raspberries and blackberries.

CURRANTS

Black-, red- and whitecurrants have a sharp, intense flavour and are picked in bunches on stems. Blackcurrants and redcurrants are most common; whitecurrants are an albino strain of redcurrants and have a less acidic flavour. High in both pectin and acid, currants need little cooking. Blackcurrants are usually made into jam, and red- and whitecurrants into jelly.

The simplest way to remove currants from the stalk is to run the prongs of a fork gently down the stalk over a bowl.

BLUEBERRIES AND BILBERRIES

Blueberries and bilberries are small, dark fruits that grow wild in Europe and the United States. Bilberries, the European species, are dark bluish black with a soft bloom. The slightly flattened sphere-shaped berries measure no more than 1cm/½in across. The larger cultivated blueberry and the wild huckleberry have a similar appearance but a sweeter flavour.

Below: Blueberries have a mild, fragrant flavour and can be made into richly coloured jams.

CRANBERRIES

Small, hard, shiny, deep red cranberries are a member of the blueberry and bilberry family. They are much too sour to eat raw but, once cooked with sugar, can be transformed into sparkling bright red jellies and rich, jam-like sauces, which are traditionally served with turkey.

GOOSEBERRIES

Popular in northern Europe, gooseberries are rarely eaten in other parts of the world. Most bushes produce hard oval berries, dark green in colour with paler stripes, and a smooth or, more usually, fuzzy skin. There is also a softer, pale purple variety.

The fruit is usually too sour to eat raw, but can be made into jellies, jams and sweet preserves. Gooseberries are rich in pectin, especially when slightly unripe, so they produce jams and jellies with a good set. Unless the mixture is being strained or sieved, they should be "topped and tailed" (trimmed) before preserving.

PHYSALIS

Also known as Cape gooseberries, although they are unrelated to gooseberries. The golden berries are enclosed in an inedible papery husk. They make good, if rather expensive, jams and bottled fruits.

Above: Tiny redcurrants have a distinctive, tart flavour and are particularly good made into sparkling jellies.

HEDGEROW FRUITS
Elderberries are the fruit of elder trees, which grow all over Europe, western Asia and the United States. The berries are small and very dark bluish black and hang in umbrella-like clusters. They can be stripped from the sprigs with a fork and are excellent preserved with crab apples or cooking apples.
Haws are the small dark berries of the hawthorn or May tree. They are slightly astringent and very good cooked with apples to make a dark red jelly.
Hips or rosehips are the orangey red fruits of the rose and can be made into a bittersweet jelly.
Sloes, a type of plum, are the fruit of the blackthorn bush, which is found in Europe and West Asia. The fruits are black with a blue bloom, and measure only about 1cm/½in across. They can be combined with apples and made into a fragrant jelly.

ORCHARD FRUITS

Apples and pears, which are available all year round, are the most common members of this family of fruits. They can be made into jams, jellies and conserves, bottled in syrup or dried into chewy rings. Other, more unusual, orchard fruits include quinces, japonicas and medlars.

APPLES

There are thousands of varieties of apples, although choice in the shops is usually limited to just a few. Among the most popular eating apples are Gala, Russet, Granny Smith, Braeburn, Golden Delicious and Cox's Orange

Below: Apples are used plentifully in jellies, jams and sweet preserves due to their high pectin content.

Above: Pears have a delicious flavour when preserved, and are equally good in tasty jams and jellies or bottled in sweet syrups.

Pippin. These all have their own individual flavours that are captured when the apples are bottled in spiced or flavoured syrup. Cooking apples are more frequently used in sweet preserves and give a good pulpy texture, although many types of eating apple are also used for their superior flavours.

Apples are high in pectin and, on their own, produce rather bland, colourless jams. They are therefore often combined with fruits with a good flavour and low pectin content to produce a jam or jelly with a better set. Using apples as a base is also a good way to make expensive fruit go further. Mild-flavoured apple jelly makes a good base for herb jellies. The jelly usually takes on a pinkish colour, so traditionally a few drops of green food colouring are added.

Most of the pectin in apples is found in the skin and seeds so apple peelings and cores are often used to make a pectin stock. This is then stirred into other fruit jams and jellies to improve their set, without affecting their flavour.

CRAB APPLES

These small apples can be gathered from the wild, from cultivated garden trees or, very occasionally, bought from independent food stores. They have a sharp, rich flavour and are very good used on their own or combined with other hedgerow fruit.

CORING APPLES AND PEARS

To core apples, place a corer over the stalk end and push it right through the fruit. Gently twist the corer and carefully pull out the core.

To core pears, start at the base of the fruit and push the corer only half way through.

To remove the core from halved fruit, scoop out the cores using a melon baller or a teaspoon to make a neat round hole.

PEARS

Unlike apples, pears are low in pectin, so are less frequently used in jams and jellies. Their sweet, mild flavour and tender texture makes them popular for jam-making and they are superb preserved in syrup or alcohol, or pickled in raspberry vinegar, either whole, halved or quartered. Pears are divided into eating and cooking varieties, although some eating pears are also suitable for cooking. The British Conference and the American Bosc are particularly good for preserving.

QUINCES

Golden yellow quinces can be the shape and size of a small squat pear or a small apple, or as large as big pears, depending on the variety. The flesh is hard, granular and sour when eaten raw, but cooking makes it smooth and tender, with a delicate tinged soft pink colour and a sherbet-like aromatic flavour. Quinces are rich in pectin and they can be made into jellies, fruit cheeses and butters; these may be a rich golden or a deep pink colour depending on the variety of quince used.

JAPONICAS

These small, round, green fruits are also known as Japanese quinces. They can be preserved in the same ways as quinces, but have a slightly sharper, lemony flavour.

Above: Medlars are not widely available but, if you can find them, they can be made into really delicious preserves.

MEDLARS

Small and brown, medlars have a squashed round shape and an open end revealing the seeds. The flesh is very hard and mouth-puckeringly acidic when first picked. To soften and sweeten the fruit, it must be "bletted" or allowed to ferment slightly. The flesh is dry and sticky and tastes a little like the flesh of dried dates. A mixture of unripe and "bletted" medlars can be made into aromatic preserves such as jams, jellies and cheeses.

Above: Quinces have a distinctive, aromatic flavour and can be made into delicious jellies, which are good spread on bread or toast.

STONE FRUITS

These are all fruits of the *Prunus* genus, recognized by their single central woody stone (pit), soft flesh and thin skin. They are well-suited to jam-making and can also be used whole or halved in bottled preserves. These fruits come in a wide variety of colours, textures and flavours, from tender pale orange apricots and yellow-skinned tart plums, to glossy sweet red cherries, and they can be made into numerous types of preserves. Plums are available all year round, and although cherries, apricots, peaches and nectarines are sometimes available at other times of the year, they are at their peak in summer and early autumn.

PLUMS

These fruits range in colour from pale gold through red and crimson to deep purple. When buying, choose firm, unwrinkled fruit, which still have a slight bloom. They will keep for several days at room temperature, but will

Below: Plums are most plentiful in the summer, so it is well worth making a batch of jam to enjoy during the rest of the year.

Above: Sweet black cherries can be made into the most delicious, richly flavoured preserves.

continue to ripen. Once they are almost ripe, they can be stored in the refrigerator for a few more days. Use them when just-ripe to make richly flavoured jams.

Mirabelle plums are a French speciality, grown particularly around Alsace. They are small, round, red-flushed yellow plums with a powerful sweet scent. They are usually preserved whole in a liqueur-enriched syrup. Greengages are small, green, fragrant plums, primarily dessert fruits, but excellent bottled or made into luxurious jams.

Purple-black damsons are available only in the early autumn months. Small and sour-tasting, they make superb jams and damson cheese. Bullaces are small, round plums that grow wild throughout Europe and can be used in the same way as damsons.

CHERRIES

These fruits are divided into two main groups: sweet cherries, which may be black (actually deep red) or white (usually yellow), and sour cherries, of which the best known are Morellos. When buying, the cherry's stem is a good indicator of freshness – it should be green and flexible not brown and brittle. Avoid any fruit that is overly soft or split. Cherries are low in pectin, so must either be combined with apples or other pectin-rich fruit, or commercial or home-made pectin stock needs to be added when making jam or other set preserves. Both sweet and sour cherries are excellent bottled in syrup.

Below: Ripe, juicy peaches are delicious preserved in sweet syrups, spirits and liqueurs.

STONING FRUITS

Large stone fruits such as peaches, nectarines, plums and apricots can all be stoned (pitted) in the same way. Cherries can also be stoned in this way, but because they are so small, it is much easier to use a special cherry stoner.

1 Using a sharp knife, carefully cut around the middle of the fruit through the crease that runs from the stem to the tip, right through to the stone.

2 Twist the halves in opposite directions to separate; the stone will remain in one of the halves.

3 To remove the stone, carefully lever it out of the fruit with a knife.

Stoning cherries To remove the stones from cherries, use a cherry stoner. Pull the stalk from the cherry, then place the fruit in the cup of the stoner and squeeze the handles of the tool together. The short prong will push through the fruit and force out the stone.

SKINNING STONE FRUITS

1 Raw peaches, nectarines and thick-skinned plums are difficult to peel with a knife. To loosen the skins, put the fruits in a heatproof bowl and pour over enough boiling water to cover.

2 Leave to stand for 1 minute, then drain and cool the fruit under cold running water. The skin should now come off easily, using the point of a small knife to peel it away.

PEACHES AND NECTARINES

A good peach or nectarine will be richly coloured and heavy, with a strong aroma. Peaches have downy skins and the most common types have yellow or pink flesh. The white-fleshed and pale-skinned variety is the sweetest of all.

Nectarines are similar to peaches but they have smooth and shiny skins and a slightly sharper taste – like a cross between a peach and a plum. They make great jams, and are good bottled in syrup or alcohol. Peaches and nectarines should be carefully skinned before making jams, jellies and sweet preserves.

APRICOTS

With their slightly sweet-and-sour flavour, soft texture and downy skins, apricots are delicious eaten fresh and raw. Cooking with sugar intensifies their flavour. Slightly under-ripe apricots can be poached in a sugar syrup with a dash of lime juice and bottled. Just-ripe fruit can be cooked with sugar to make jams.

Right: Smooth-skinned nectarines can be preserved in the same way as peaches.

Apricots and almonds are a very popular combination and split almonds can be added to special conserves for extra flavour and texture. When choosing apricots, pick those with the strongest colour for the sweetest flavour.

CITRUS FRUITS

With their aromatic acidity, citrus fruits are the main ingredient of nearly all marmalades and fruit curds. They are also often added to other preserves because they have a high pectin and acid content, and they are frequently used in jams and jellies to help achieve a good set. Their pungency and sharpness adds not only flavour but also offsets sweetness. Members of the citrus family include lemons, limes, oranges, grapefruits and tangerines as well as the more exotic ugli fruit, citrons and kumquats, and hybrids such as the clementine and limequat. All are covered in a thick peel, which consists mainly of white pith and a colourful outer layer of zest or rind.

Below: Sweet, juicy oranges are most commonly preserved as tangy breakfast marmalades.

ORANGES

There are three types of sweet oranges: the common orange is a medium-size fruit with a fine-grained skin, and popular varieties are Valencia, Jaffa and Shamouti, which is available only in the winter. These are the juiciest oranges and are ideal for sweet marmalades and orange curds. They often contain a lot of pips (seeds), which are essential for marmalade-making because they are high in pectin.

Navel oranges are seedless, so are better preserved whole, in segments or in slices. Red-flushed blood oranges have ruby-coloured flesh and a rich, almost berry-like flavour. These make excellent marmalade when combined with sharper lemons, but are less successful for curd-making because their deeply coloured juice looks rather unappetizing when mixed with yellow butter and eggs.

Bitter Seville oranges have a high pectin and acid content, as well as an excellent, punchy flavour and make the finest marmalades. (The bulk of the Spanish crop is exported to Britain for this purpose.) The season is a fairly short one and they are only available for a few weeks during the winter. However, bitter oranges can be successfully frozen whole or chopped. Alternatively, the oranges can be chopped and cooked without sugar until very soft before cooling and freezing. When ready to use, they can be thawed and then boiled with sugar to setting point.

Above: Sharp, zesty lemons are widely used in curds, marmalades and sweet preserves.

LEMONS

In the preserving kitchen, lemons are indispensable. They add acid and pectin to jams and jellies made from low-pectin fruit such as strawberries and peaches, which are difficult to set. Adding lemon juice to jellies also gives them a sparkling appearance. A dash of lemon juice added to preserves made from soft fruit such as strawberries and exotic fruits such as papayas, helps bring out their flavour. A few spoonfuls of lemon juice added to cold water makes an acidulated dip that will prevent cut fruit such as pears and apples from discolouring.

Small, thin-skinned lemons are juicier, so are perfect for making curds; bigger, more knobbly ones have a higher proportion of peel and pith to flesh, so are better for marmalades and candying.

Above: Limes have a distinctive, sharp flavour and are delicious made into sweet marmalades or blended with other fruits.

LIMES

These small green fruits flourish in near-tropical conditions. They have a distinctive, tangy flavour and are one of the most sour citrus fruits. A squeeze of lime juice can be added to jams and jellies instead of lemon juice to enhance the flavour of the fruit and to improve the set. It goes particularly well with tropical fruits, such as mangoes and papayas.

Right: Tiny orange kumquats look delightful preserved in syrup.

GRAPEFRUITS

One of the largest citrus fruits, with a diameter of up to 15cm/6in. The flesh of grapefruits varies in colour from pale yellow to the dark reddish pink of sweeter ruby grapefruit. The yellow skinned and fleshed varieties have a sharp and refreshing flavour that makes good marmalade. Sweetie grapefruits are a less sharp variety with a vibrant bright green skin.

CITRONS

This large, lemon-shaped fruit grows to 20cm/8in in length. It has a fairly thick lumpy greenish yellow peel that is often candied and is used in commercial candied peel. The very sour-tasting pulp is sometimes made into sweet preserves, but it has no other culinary use.

POMELOS

Also known as the shaddock, this large citrus fruit resembles a pear-shaped grapefruit. The flesh can be used to make jams and the rind can be candied with sugar or used to make marmalade.

Left: Pink grapefruits have a milder flavour than yellow ones and can be made into very pretty preserves.

TANGERINES AND MANDARIN ORANGES

These are the generic names for small, flat citrus fruits with loose skins and a sweet or tart-sweet flavour. Satsumas, clementines and mineolas also fall into this group. Satsumas are slightly tart and very juicy; clementines (a cross between the tangerine and the bitter orange) are similar but have a thinner, more tight-fitting skin. Both fruits are almost seedless so are the best choice for preserving whole in sugar syrup. Mineolas are larger. They are hybrids of the grapefruit and tangerine, have a sharp, tangy flavour and resemble oranges in size and colour.

KUMQUATS AND LIMEQUATS

The tiny, orange, oval kumquat with its distinctive sweet-sour flavour can be eaten whole and unpeeled; the rind has a sweeter flavour than the flesh. Kumquats are delicious pickled, preserved in syrup or candied.

Limequats are a cross between a lime and a kumquat. The small, bright green fruits have a fragrant flavour and can be preserved in the same way as kumquats, although they have a slightly more sour flavour. The two fruits look very pretty bottled together in the same jar and make a lovely gift.

HYBRID FRUITS

There are a huge number of citrus hybrids that are bred for flavour, colour or to be seedless.

ugli fruit

Available in winter, this hybrid of the grapefruit, tangerine and orange has a loose, rough, greeny yellow skin and a slightly squashed appearance. It is very juicy and sweet and can be used instead of grapefruit in marmalades. The peel is very good candied.

temple oranges

These loose-skinned fruits are a cross between a tangerine and an orange. Slightly oval in shape, they have rough, thick, deep orange skin, which makes them popular for marmalade-making in the United States. The flesh is sweet, yet tart and contains a fair number of seeds. Temple oranges are in season from December to March.

BUYING AND STORING

Look for firm, plump citrus fruits that feel heavy for their size as this indicates that the fruit will be juicy. Avoid dry, wrinkled specimens, soft squashy fruit or any with brown spots. Green patches on lemons and yellow patches on limes are a sign of immaturity.

Citrus fruits can be kept at room temperature for several days, but for longer storage, keep them in the refrigerator, putting unwaxed fruit in a plastic bag. Always wash and scrub citrus fruits before using them in preserves.

GRATING CITRUS RIND
To make long, thin shreds, scrape a canelle knife or zester along the surface of the fruit, applying firm pressure.

To make finer shreds, gently rub the fruit over the fine side of a grater to remove the rind without taking off any bitter white pith. Use a dry pastry brush to brush off any rind that sticks to the grater.

CUTTING RIND INTO FINE STRIPS OR JULIENNE

1 Using a vegetable peeler or a sharp knife, remove strips of rind as thinly as possible, without taking off any of the bitter white pith.

2 Stack several strips of rind on top of each other and, using a sharp knife, cut them into fine strips or julienne.

FLAVOURING SUGAR
To add a hint of citrus flavour to a preserve, rub the fruit's skin with 1 or 2 sugar cubes, turning the cubes as each side becomes saturated with the oil. Weigh the cubes with the sugar.

PEELING CITRUS FRUIT
1 To peel large citrus fruit such as grapefruit, cut a slice from the top and bottom of the fruit, through the flesh, then cut away the rind, pith and skin, working from top to base, following the curve of the fruit.

2 To peel smaller fruits such as oranges, cut off the rind, pith and skin in a long spiral.

SEGMENTING CITRUS FRUIT
1 Holding the peeled fruit in one hand and the knife in the other, slice the knife down one side of a segment, cutting it away from the membrane. Cut down the other side and pull out the segment.

2 Repeat with the remaining segments, turning back the flaps of membrane like a book. When all the segments are removed, squeeze the remaining fruit to extract the juice.

TROPICAL FRUITS

With imports from many parts of the world, tropical fruits are now available all year round, but tend to be at their best during the winter months. They are often vibrantly coloured with fabulous flavours and make fragrant jams and luxurious sweet preserves.

PINEAPPLES

This distinctive fruit has extremely juicy, sweet and refreshing golden flesh. It can be made into lovely jams and jellies, which are ideal for serving with chicken, pork and ham. Pineapple rings are also good candied or preserved in syrup.

Once picked, pineapples do not ripen so always buy ripe fruits. (If you do buy an unripe fruit, leaving it for a few days may help reduce the acidity.) Ripe fruits should give off a sweet aroma and be orange all over with no brown parts. They can be stored in a cool place for up to a week.

PREPARING A PINEAPPLE

1 Using a sharp knife, slice off the base and plume of the pineapple. Rest the cut base on a board. Cut away the peel thinly, working from the top downwards, then cut out the "eyes" following their spiral around the fruit.

2 To make pineapple rings, cut the peeled fruit into thick slices, then remove the central core from each slice using a 2cm/¾in round cookie cutter.

GUAVAS

These fruits have a sweet, almost spicy aroma and flavour, with granular flesh that becomes creamy when ripe. The small oval fruits, no larger than 7.5cm/3in long, have a number of small seeds in the centre. Buy fruits with smooth skins and no wrinkling or brown patches around the stalk. Guavas will keep for a few days in the refrigerator but always wrap them in clear film (plastic wrap) because their aroma will permeate other foods. Peel them thinly, then halve and remove the seeds. They can be made into fragrant jams, cheeses and sparkling jellies, with a honey-like aroma, and pink or gold colour, depending on the variety used. It is essential to add lemon or lime juice to preserves that are made with guavas to achieve a good set and to heighten the flavour.

PAPAYAS

Also known as pawpaw, these pear-shaped fruits have a green skin that turns a speckled yellow when the fruit is ripe. The creamy textured flesh is a vibrant orange-pink colour with a wonderful sweet flavour and an exquisite perfumed aroma. To prepare papayas, cut them in half lengthways and gently scoop out the numerous black seeds. Make sure that the fruit is just ripe to make the best jams and butters.

Right: Pineapples have a sweet, sharp, tangy flavour and are good in jellies, jams and tangy relishes.

MANGOES

The skins of these luscious fruits range in colour from green, through yellow and orange to red. Ripe fruits have deep-orange flesh, which will yield slightly when the uncut fruit is gently squeezed. Just-ripe and green under-ripe mangoes can be made into excellent, highly flavoured jams, but over-ripe fruit should be avoided as mangoes tend to become more fibrous when very ripe and soft. When mangoes are scarce or expensive, substitute up to half the total weight of mangoes with cooking apples.

BANANAS

These long, yellow fruits make delicious, though not particularly attractive, jams. Their sweet flavour and soft, pulpy texture combine well with dried fruits such as dates and figs, which need a relatively short cooking time. It is best to use just-ripe bananas for jams and sweet

PREPARING A MANGO
The simplest way to prepare a mango is to remove the skin with a vegetable peeler and slice the flesh off the stone (pit). To cut mango flesh into cubes, use the following method.

1 Hold the mango with one hand and cut vertically down one side of the stone. Repeat on the other side.

2 Cut into the flesh, but not all the way through the peel, lengthways and widthways.

3 Holding the mango slices with the flesh side upwards, press each slice inside out, opening the cuts in the flesh. Cut the mango cubes from the peel. Cut any remaining flesh from the stone, remove the peel and cube.

preserves; choose ones with smooth, yellow skins that have only a few brown speckles and discard any soft brown flesh that may have been bruised.

Dried bananas are sun-dried in their skins, then peeled to reveal dark, sticky fruit inside. They have a concentrated flavour and can add sweetness. Do not confuse them with banana chips, which are hard, dried slices of banana, unsuitable for using in preserves.

Below: Fragrant mangoes are fabulous made into sweet jams and jellies.

Plantains, another member of the banana family, are "cooking" bananas. Green-skinned with flecks of brown, turning black when fully ripe, they may retain much of their shape after cooking and are good in jams and sweet preserves.

Above: Although not traditionally throught of as a preserving fruit, bananas can be made into surprisingly good jams.

Left: Kiwi fruits can be made into delicious pale green jams or blended with other fruits.

KIWI FRUITS

Although completely unrelated to the gooseberry, these fuzzy, brown, egg-shaped fruits were once known as Chinese gooseberries. The flesh is bright green with a sunray pattern of black seeds. Just-ripe fruit (when it yields to gentle pressure) should be used for jam-making. Kiwi fruit has a slightly sharp flavour so it is usually better to use sugar with pectin than to add lemon juice to get a good set.

PASSION FRUITS

These oval fruits have leathery reddish purple skins that become dimpled when the fruit is ripe. Inside are small, hard edible seeds, surrounded by fragrant, intensely flavoured orange pulp. The pulp and seeds may be scooped out of halved passion fruit shells and made into jam. Alternatively, the pulp can be rubbed through a fine sieve with a spoonful of boiling water to extract the juice, leaving the seeds behind. The juice can then be used with other fruit to make intensely flavoured, aromatic jams, jellies and curds.

Grenadillas are a larger, but less fragrant, member of this fruit family.

PERSIMMONS AND SHARON FRUIT

Rather like squarish, squashed tomatoes in shape, persimmons have a deep orange, smooth and shiny skin, and are about 6cm/2½in in diameter. Before they are ripe, the flesh has an astringent taste and pithy texture. The fruits tend to ripen suddenly, transforming into a soft, sweet fruit with no trace of bitterness. This quality encouraged the growers to develop the Sharon fruit, a golden-orange persimmon that is almost entirely seedless and sweet even when firm. The skins are tough, so the fruit should be peeled before making into jam, but this is not necessary when making jellies.

TAMARILLOS

This egg-shaped fruit of the tomato family (sometimes known as a "tree tomato"), may be yellow, red, or dark red; the yellow variety has the finest flavour. Tamarillos can be made into exotic sweet jellies that are ideal for special occasions. The skin has a very bitter taste so the fruit should be peeled beforehand. This can be made easier by blanching the fruits first to loosen their skins.

POMEGRANATES

The shape and size of an orange, pomegranates have tough, leathery skin and a large calyx, and range in colour from deep yellow to crimson. Inside are dozens of white seeds surrounded by transluscent pinkish red flesh, encased in a cream-coloured membrane. The seeds, pith and membranes are bitter so it is the juice that is extracted to make jams and jellies. The simplest way to do this is to cut the fruit in half and use a lemon squeezer to squeeze out the juice, taking care not to crush the seeds. Grenadine, a sweet syrup used in cocktails and mixed drinks, is made from pomegranate juice, and a dash of this can be used to flavour preserves.

Below: The bright pink flesh of pomegranates can be made into beautiful glistening jellies.

MELONS, GRAPES, DATES AND FIGS

These fruits don't fit into any particular category but are all popular in jam- and preserve-making. They were among the first to be cultivated and originate from different parts of the globe. They come in a vast array of shapes, sizes and colours, each with a distinct flavour and texture that can be made into sumptuous jams and preserves.

MELONS

There are two kinds of melon: the dessert melon and the watermelon. Dessert melons may have green or yellow skins, sometimes streaky or netted (with fibrous markings), and fragrant, dense flesh, ranging from pale greens and yellows to deep orange. Most are ripe if they yield under your thumb when pressed on the stem end. They should also give off a sweet aroma, especially close to the stem end. Once ripe, they should be kept in a cool place and used within a few days. When cut they will keep for a day or two in the refrigerator, and should be covered with clear film to keep the lfesh moist. The flavour of melon in preserves is not intense. They work well if combined with strong flavourings such as ginger, or other fruits such as pineapple, passion fruit, peach and mango. They are also good scooped into balls with a melon baller or cut into cubes

Left: The orange flesh of cantaloupe melons is excellent scooped into balls and preserved in a sweet syrup.

Above: Juicy black grapes are good for making into delicate, fragrant, sparkling jellies.

and preserved in syrup or alcohol. Watermelons have a high water content, at around 90 per cent, so the flesh is not ideal for use in jams and preserves.

GRAPES

Of the many grape varieties that are available, the smaller seedless grapes are preferable for preserves as they need less preparation and have thin skins with little tannin.

RHUBARB

Technically, rhubarb is the stem of a vegetable. Outdoor-grown rhubarb is available in late spring and has crimson and green stems. It can be used for jams. Forced rhubarb, cultivated indoors without light, has thin, tender, pale stems and makes more delicately flavoured jams and jellies. Rhubarb has a very sharp, intense flavour and goes particularly well with orange and ginger.

Above: Naturally sweet, dates make the perfect addition to flavoursome jams.

Usually, grapes are referred to as either black or white, although the colours vary a great deal from pale green to pinkish red and dark purplish black. Grape flavours range from honey-sweet to sharp and bitter and can be almost lemon-scented. When buying, choose fruits that are firm with smooth skin and no sign of turning brown near the stem end. Store them in the refrigerator and bring to room temperature before using. Grapes make good jams and jellies, sometimes flavoured with alcohol such as wine.

DATES

Plump and glossy, fresh dates are soft and packed with concentrated sugar. The thin papery skins should be slipped off and the long stone (pit) removed before the flesh is added to jams and preserves. When the date is squeezed at the stem end, the succulent ripe flesh should pop easily out of the skin, after which you can use a sharp knife to cut the fruit in half and carefully prise out the inner stone.

FIGS

These fragile fruits have thin skins that may be purple or greenish gold; inside is a glorious soft, scented flesh filled with tiny round seeds. Fresh figs need careful handling as they damage easily. When figs are ripe and yield to a light pressure, they can be poached whole in syrup for bottling; they do not need to be peeled, simply snip off the tough stem. Avoid sour-smelling figs; this indicates they are over-ripe. When figs are plentiful, they can be made into luxurious conserves and jams. Warm spices such as cinnamon and vanilla go very well with figs. Dried figs, with their concentrated flavour, make a thick, dark and delicious jam. A little grated orange rind added to the mixture heightens the flavour.

DRIED FRUITS

All kinds of fruits are available dried and they can successfully be made into jams and sweet preserves. Jams made with dried fruits have a concentrated fruity flavour and often require less sugar than fresh fruit jams. Modern tenderized dried fruit, often labelled "ready-to-eat", requires a short soaking time, or sometimes none at all, before being made into jam. Any soaking liquid may be used as part of the recipe. If the fruit needs to be chopped into small pieces, do this after soaking, or it will absorb too much water.

Dried figs are wonderful steeped in sweet syrups, often flavoured with a liqueur such as Cointreau or Grand Marnier. Prunes also make good preserves, either on their own in syrup or alcohol, or blended with other ingredients to make excellent jams.

Below: Figs have a subtle, sweet flavour and are particularly good bottled whole in syrup.

SPICES, HERBS AND FLOWERS

Flavourings are an essential part of most preserves and using the right amount is as important as selecting the correct one.

SPICES

These are used in all kinds of preserves both for flavour and decoration.

Allspice With an aroma and flavour that is reminiscent of cloves, cinnamon and nutmeg, this is good used with orchard fruits.

Cassia and cinnamon The bark is available ground or in sticks. The sticks are best used whole for flavouring pale or clear preserves.

Cloves These tiny dried flower buds, sold whole or ground, have a distinctive taste that goes well with apples and citrus fruit.

Below: Vanilla, star anise, ground ginger and cinnamon sticks are all widely used in preserves.

Ginger Good in sweet preserves, root ginger may be used fresh, dried or ground to add a tangy spiciness. Preserved stem ginger can be added to conserves and marmalades.

Juniper Used to give gin its distinctive flavour, blue-black juniper berries may be used fresh, but are more usually dried.

Nutmeg and mace Nutmeg has a warm nutty flavour. It is best bought whole and grated fresh. Mace is the orange-coloured lacy outer covering of the nutmeg; it is sold as blades.

Star anise This star-shaped, aniseed-flavoured spice looks wonderful in bottled preserves.

Vanilla Used to flavour bottled fruits and occasionally jams and jellies, long, dark brown vanilla pods (beans) have a sweet, warm, aromatic flavour. The pods can be re-used if rinsed thoroughly, dried and stored in an airtight jar.

HERBS AND FLOWERS

Herbs and flowers can added during the inital cooking, then removed, or finely chopped and stirred in towards the end.

Borage The tiny, brilliant blue or purple flowers of this plant can be candied or used to decorate jellies. Borage leaves have a fresh cucumber-like taste and can be used to flavour jellies.

Geranium leaves These give jams and jellies a subtle flavour. There are several different varieties with apple, rose or lemon aromas.

Kaffir lime leaf This strong-tasting, aromatic leaf is used to flavour

Above: Whole cinnamon sticks are often used to flavour sweet syrups for preserving fruits.

Thai and Malaysian preserves.

Lavender Intensely fragrant, sprigs of lavender can be used to flavour sugar, jams and jellies. The sprigs also look very pretty suspended in jelly: dip them in boiling water first, then shake off the excess before putting them in the jar and pouring over the hot jelly.

Lemon grass This tall hard grass, with a distinctive lemony taste, is used in Thai preserves.

Mint The many varieties of this aromatic herb include peppermint, spearmint, apple mint, lemon mint and pineapple mint. It adds a fresh flavour to preserves, but should be used sparingly.

Rose Scented red, pink or yellow petals make wonderful jams and jellies. They are often combined with fruit juice, such as grape, and with added pectin, so that the preserve sets quickly without destroying the aroma of the petals.

PRESERVING INGREDIENTS

Preserving ingredients prolong the life of the other ingredients used in a preserve by creating an environment in which micro-organisms such as moulds and bacteria cannot grow.

SUGAR

This is the key preservative used in jams, jellies, marmalades, curds and many preserved fruits. A high proportion of sugar is needed and if the sugar content is less than 60 per cent of the total weight of the preserve (for example, in low-sugar jams), this will affect the keeping quality. Low-sugar jams should be used within a few months and kept in the refrigerator.

Sugar also plays an important role in the setting of jams. To achieve a good set, sugar should make up between 55 and 70 per cent of the total weight of the preserve. (High acid content in the fruit makes the exact amount of sugar less crucial.)

white sugars

These refined sugars produce clear, set, sweet preserves.

Preserving sugar has quite large, irregular crystals and is ideal for jams, jellies and marmalades. The large crystals allow water to percolate between them, which helps to prevent burning and reduces the need for stirring (which is important to avoid breaking up fruit too much). Use this sugar for the clearest preserves. If you cannot find preserving sugar, granulated sugar can be used instead.

Preserving sugar with pectin Also known as jam sugar, this sugar is used with low-pectin fruit. The sugar contains natural pectin and citric acid to help overcome setting problems. Preserves made with this sugar tend to have a shorter shelf-life and should be stored for no longer than six months.

Granulated sugar is less coarse than preserving sugar, but still less expensive and gives a clear result.

brown sugars

These sugars give a pronounced flavour and darker colour to jams and preserves.

Demerara/raw sugar is a pale golden sugar with a mild caramel flavour. Traditionally an unrefined sugar with a low molasses content, it may also be made from refined white sugar with molasses added.

Golden granulated sugar may be refined or unrefined. It can be used instead of white sugar for a hint of flavour and colour.

Soft brown sugar is moist, with fine grains and a rich flavour. It may be light or dark in colour and is usually made from refined white sugar with molasses added.

Muscovado/molasses sugar may be light or dark and is usually made from unrefined cane sugar. It has a deeper, more pronounced taste than soft brown sugar.

Palm sugar is made from the sap of palms and has a fragrant flavour that is ideal for preserves that use flowers. Sold pressed into blocks, it needs to be chopped before use. Light muscovado (brown) sugar is a good alternative.

Jaggery is a raw sugar from India with a distinctive taste. It must be chopped before use. Use a mixture of light muscovado and demerara sugar as an alternative.

ALCOHOL

Spirits, such as brandy and rum, and liqueurs, which are at least 40% ABV (alcohol by volume), can be used. Fortified wine, wine, beer and cider have a lower alcohol content so are not effective alone and should be either heat treated or combined with sugar.

Below: White and golden sugars are a key ingredient used in sweet fruit preserves, jams and jellies.

EQUIPMENT

While very few specialist items are essential for preserving, having the correct equipment for the job will make the whole process easier and helps to ensure success. You will probably have most of the basic items such as a large heavy pan, weighing scales or calibrated measuring cups, wooden spoons, a chopping board and a few sharp knives. However, a few specific items such as a jam funnel for potting preserves and a jelly bag for straining fruit juices will prove invaluable. The following is a brief outline of the more useful items, all of which are readily available from large department stores and specialist kitchen equipment stores.

PRESERVING PAN

A preserving pan or large, heavy pan is essential. It must be of a sufficient size to allow rapid boiling without bubbling over (a capacity of about 9 litres/ 16 pints/8 quarts is ideal); wide enough to allow rapid evaporation of liquid, so that setting point is reached quickly; and have a thick heavy base to protect the preserve from burning. Preserving pans are fitted with a pair of short-looped handles, or a carrying handle over the top. A non-corrosive preserving pan such as one made of stainless steel is the best choice for making all types of preserves, and they are also readily available and inexpensive. Traditional copper preserving pans, usually very wide at the top and sloping to a narrow base, are intended only for jam- and jelly-making and are

unsuitable for preserves containing lemon juice, or for acidic or red fruit, as both the flavour and colour will be spoilt. Enamel pans are not ideal as they do not conduct heat fast enough for preserving and they burn easily.

SUGAR THERMOMETER

Invaluable for cooking preserves to the exact temperature needed for a perfect set. Choose a thermometer that goes up to at least 110°C/ 230°F, and has a clip or a handle that can be attached to the pan, so that it does not slip into the boiling preserve.

JELLY BAG

Used to strain fruit juices from cooked fruit pulp for jelly-making, jelly bags are made from calico, cotton flannel or nylon. The close weave allows only the fruit juice to flow through, leaving the pulp behind. Some jelly bags have their own stands; others have loops with which to suspend the bag.

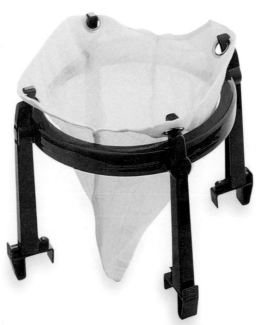

MUSLIN/CHEESECLOTH

Used for making spice and herb bags, muslin is also useful for tying together pips and peel, particularly when making marmalade. It can also be used instead of a jelly bag. To do this, layer three or four squares of muslin together and tie lengths of strong string (twine) securely to each corner. Either knot the ends together to hang from a single support, or make four loops so the bag can be suspended on the legs of an upturned stool or chair. Alternatively, line a large strainer with the muslin squares and place over a bowl to catch the juices.

JARS AND BOTTLES

When making preserves, a selection of containers is needed. Clear glass is ideal because it is non-corrosive, you can easily check for trapped air bubbles when potting preserves, and it looks very pretty when filled. As well as ordinary jam jars and bottles, there are specialist preserving jars that are designed to be heated to a high temperature. Non-corrosive seals are essential, particularly when potting more acidic preserves.

Be sure to choose appropriately shaped and sized containers. Wide-necked jars are essential for recipes using whole or large pieces of fruit, but for most preserves it is better to use several smaller jars than one or two large ones.

Left: A jelly bag with its own stand can make an easy job of straining jellies.

Preserves stored in very large jars are likely to deteriorate more quickly once the seal is broken; the preserve is not consumed as quickly and the contents are exposed to the air for longer than a preserve stored in a small jar.

PRESERVE COVERS

The cheapest way to cover jams, jellies and marmalades is to use a waxed paper disc and cellophane cover, secured by a rubber band; these covers are available to fit 450g/1lb and 900g/2lb jars. They are very easy to handle and use: simply lay the wax disc over the jam, jelly or marmalade in the jar and then secure the cellophane cover over the entire top of the jar with a rubber band, making it airtight.

HYDROMETER

Also known as a *pèse syrop*, a hydrometer measures the density of sugar syrup and is sometimes used when bottling fruit and for jam- and jelly-making. The tube is marked from 0 to 40 and measures the point to which the weighted tube sinks. The more sugar a syrup contains, the higher the hydrometer will float in it.

FUNNELS

These make potting preserves considerably easier. A jam funnel with a wide tube (10–13cm/4–5in diameter) that fits into the top of the jar or container can make quick, clean work of filling jars.

An ordinary funnel with a slimmer tube is useful for adding liquid to jars of fruit as well as for bottling smooth sauces and jellies. Some funnels have inner attachments that allow you to filter or strain the liquid while you are pouring. This can be useful for catching small pieces, although a proper strainer would be needed for more heavy filtering. Choose funnels made of heatproof plastic or stainless steel.

Above: A jam funnel can prove to be a real time-saver when potting jellies, jams and conserves.

Below: A selection of jars with either clamp-top, screw-top or two-piece screw-band lids are perfect for preserving.

POTTING AND COVERING PRESERVES

Make sure you have enough jars and bottles, and the correct sterilizing equipment, before you start to make any preserve.

CHOOSING CONTAINERS

To make the most of preserves, always pot them in the right type of container. It is better to pack preserves into several smaller containers rather than one large one, especially those that need to be consumed soon after opening.

Screw-top lidded jars are suitable for most sweet preserves. Clamp-top jars are also good as they produce an airtight vacuum that improves storage.

STERILIZING JARS AND BOTTLES

Before potting, it is essential to sterilize jars and bottles to destroy any micro-organisms in containers. Check jars and bottles for cracks

or damage, then wash thoroughly in hot, soapy water, rinse well and turn upside-down to drain. Jars and bottles may be sterilized in five different ways: by heating in a low oven, immersing in boiling water, heating in a microwave, hot-washing in a dishwasher, or using sterilizing tablets.

oven method

Stand the containers, spaced slightly apart, on a baking sheet lined with kitchen paper. Rest any lids on top. Place in a cold oven, then heat to 110°C/225°F/Gas ¼ and bake for 30 minutes. Leave to cool slightly before filling. (If the jars or bottles are not used immediately, cover with a clean cloth and warm again before use.)

Below: Medium, wide-necked jars with plastic-coated screw-top lids are ideal for most preserves.

dishwasher method

This is the simplest way to clean and sterilize a large number of containers at the same time. Put the containers and lids in a dishwasher and run it on its hottest setting, including drying. If the jars are already washed and clean, you can run the cycle without adding detergent.

boiling water method

1 Place the containers, open-end up, in a deep pan that is wide enough to hold them in one layer.

2 Pour enough hot water into the pan to cover the containers. (Do not use boiling water because this can crack glass.) Bring the water to the boil and boil for 10 minutes.

3 Leave the containers in the pan until the water stops bubbling, then carefully remove and drain upside-down on a clean dishtowel. Turn the containers upright and leave to air-dry for a few minutes.

4 Immerse lids, seals and corks in simmering water for 20 seconds. (Only ever use corks once.)

microwave method

This method is particularly useful when sterilizing only a few jars for potting a small amount of preserve. It is also quick and easy, so it is a useful method to use if you have limited time. Follow the microwave manufacturer's instructions and only use for jars that hold less than 450g/1lb and short squat bottles.

1 Half fill the clean jars or bottles with water and heat on full power until the water has boiled for at least 1 minute.

2 Using oven gloves, remove the jars or bottles from the microwave. Carefully swirl the water inside them, then pour it away. Drain upside-down on a clean dishtowel, then turn upright and leave to dry.

sterilizing tablet method

This easy-to-use method is not suitable for delicately flavoured preserves because the tablets may leave a slight taste. However, it is fine for robustly flavoured preserves. Following the instructions on the packet, dissolve the tablets and soak the containers in the sterilizing solution. Drain and dry thoroughly before use.

FILLING JARS

Most preserves should be potted into hot containers as soon as they are ready. Whole fruit jams, marmalades with peel, and jellies with added ingredients such as fresh herbs should be left to cool for 10 minutes until a thin skin forms on the surface. The preserve should then be stirred to distribute the ingredients and prevent them sinking once potted.

Different types of preserves need to be covered and sealed in different ways. Jams, conserves, jellies, marmalades and fruit cheeses can be covered with a waxed paper disc and the jar covered with cellophane held in place with a rubber band. Or the jar can be sealed with a screw-top lid. (Waxed discs and cellophane covers should not be used together with a screw-top lid.)

Bottled fruits must be sealed in jars with new rubber seals and vacuum or clamp-top lids. The latter are easy to use and very effective for keeping air out. They are readily available, although more costly than regular jars.

using waxed discs and cellophane covers

1 Using a heat-resistant ladle or jug (pitcher) and a jam funnel, carefully fill the jars with hot jam, almost to the top. Leave a small space of no more than 1cm/½in.

2 Using a clean, damp cloth, wipe the rim of the jar, making sure there are no dribbles of jam.

3 Place a waxed paper disc (waxed side down) on top of the preserve and smooth it down to form a good fit over the hot preserve.

4 Moisten a cellophane disc with a damp cloth and place on the jar, moist side up, then secure with an elastic band. Do this either when the preserve is very hot, or leave it to cool completely. (If sealed while warm, mould will grow on the surface.) As it dries, the cellophane will shrink, creating a tight seal.

MAKING JAMS, JELLIES AND MARMALADES

These are made from fruit boiled with sugar until setting point is reached. They rely on pectin, sugar and acid for a good set. Pectin is a natural, gum-like substance, which is essential in jam-, jelly- and marmalade-making. Found in the cores, pips (seeds), pith and skins of fruits, it reacts with sugar and acid to form the gel that helps to set jams, jellies and marmalades.

testing pectin content

Pectin content can vary according to the variety of fruit, when it is picked, and growing conditions. It is best to test for pectin content at an early stage in jam-making, and add extra pectin if necessary.

1 To test for pectin content, cook the fruit until soft, then spoon 5ml/1 tsp of the juices into a glass. Add 15ml/1 tbsp methylated spirits (denatured alcohol) and shake.

2 After 1 minute a clot should form: one large jelly-like clot indicates high pectin content; two or three small clots indicate the pectin content is medium and should achieve a set; lots of small clots, or no clots at all indicate low pectin content and that extra pectin will be needed for a set.

3 If the pectin content is medium, add 15ml/1 tbsp lemon juice for every 450g/1lb fruit. If the pectin content is low, add 75–90ml/5–6 tbsp pectin stock for every 450g/1lb fruit. Alternatively, add pectin powder or liquid, or use sugar containing pectin.

making pectin stock

Home-made pectin stock is very easy to make and can be stirred into low-pectin fruit jams and jellies to improve their set. Stir in after the initial cooking of the fruit and before the sugar is added. A teaspoon of the juices can be taken from the pan at this stage and tested for pectin content.

1 Roughly chop 900g/2lb cooking apples, including the cores, peel and pips. Place in a large heavy pan and pour over cold water to cover. Bring to the boil, then reduce the heat, cover and simmer for 40 minutes, or until very soft.

2 Pour the mixture into a sterilized jelly bag suspended over a bowl. Leave to drain for at least 2 hours.

3 Pour the drained juices into the cleaned pan and boil for about 20 minutes, or until the volume is reduced by one-third.

4 Pour the pectin stock into 150ml/¼ pint/⅔ cup sterilized containers and store in the refrigerator for up to 1 week or freeze for up to 4 months.

5 To use frozen pectin stock, defrost at room temperature, or overnight in the refrigerator, then stir into the preserve.

TESTING FOR A SET
Some preserves reach setting point quickly, so check early in the cooking time.

Wrinkle test Remove the preserve from the heat and spoon a little preserve on to a chilled plate. Leave to cool for 1 minute, then push the preserve with a finger; the top should wrinkle. If it wrinkles only slightly, return the preserve to the heat and cook for 2 minutes more, then test again.

Flake test Coat a spoon in the preserve; cool for a few seconds, then hold the spoon horizontally. When shaken, the jam should run off the side in one flat flake.

Thermometer test Briefly stir the preserve, dip a jam thermometer into very hot water, then place in the preserve. Move it around, but do not touch the pan base. Jams and marmalades reach setting point at 105°C/220°F; jellies and conserves a degree lower.

MAKING JAM

Usually made with whole or cut fruit, jam should have distinct flavour, bright colour and soft set.

making summer fruit jam

Use sound, slightly under-ripe fruit; over-ripe fruit contains less pectin and will not set well.

Makes about 1.6kg/3½lb

INGREDIENTS

900g/2lb mixed fruits, such as cherries, raspberries, strawberries, gooseberries, blackcurrants and redcurrants

2.5–20ml/½–4 tsp lemon juice

900g/2lb/4½ cups preserving or granulated sugar

1 Weigh each type of fruit, then prepare. Rinse and drain cherries, gooseberries, blackcurrants and redcurrants; wash raspberries and strawberries only if necessary; remove any stems and leaves and cut off any damaged parts.

2 Put the lemon juice in a large heavy pan: strawberries and cherries are low in pectin, so add 10ml/2 tsp lemon juice for each 450g/1lb fruit; add 2.5ml/½ tsp for each 450g/1lb raspberries; and add no lemon juice for high-pectin gooseberries and currants.

3 Put the prepared gooseberries, blackcurrants and redcurrants in the pan with 60ml/4 tbsp water and cook over a low heat for 5 minutes until the skins soften.

4 Add the raspberries, cherries and strawberries to the pan. (If using only these fruits, do not add any water.) Cook for 10 minutes until all the fruit is just tender.

5 Using the back of a spoon, crush one-third of the fruit to release the pectin. If using a high proportion of strawberries or cherries, do a pectin test at this stage.

6 Add the sugar to the pan and stir over a low heat until it has dissolved completely. Increase the heat and bring to the boil. Continue to boil rapidly for about 10 minutes, stirring occasionally, until setting point is reached (105°C/220°F). Skim off any froth that rises to the surface.

7 Remove the pan from the heat and leave to stand for 5 minutes. If necessary, skim off any froth, then stir to distribute larger pieces of fruit. Pot, seal and label.

making seedless raspberry jam

Some fruits, notably raspberries and blackberries, contain a large number of pips (seeds), which result in a very "pippy" jam or conserve. If you prefer a smooth jam without pips, they can be removed after initial cooking by pressing the fruit through a nylon or stainless steel sieve (strainer).

Makes about 750g/1⅔lb

INGREDIENTS

450g/1lb/2⅔ cups raspberries

about 450g/1lb/2¼ cups preserving or granulated sugar

1 Use a mixture of just-ripe and a few slightly underripe berries to ensure a good set. Put the fruit in a large heavy pan and gently crush to release the juices using the back of a wooden spoon.

2 Gently heat the fruit mixture to boiling point, then simmer for about 10 minutes, stirring now and then, until the fruit is really soft.

3 Pour the mixture into a fine nylon or stainless steel sieve placed over a bowl and push through the fruit purée using the back of the wooden spoon. Discard the pips left in the sieve.

4 Measure the fruit pulp into the cleaned pan, adding 450g/1lb/ 2¼ cups sugar for each 600ml/ 1 pint/2½ cups purée. Heat gently, stirring, until the sugar dissolves, then boil rapidly until setting point is reached (105°C/220°F).

5 Using a slotted spoon, skim any froth from the surface, then pot the jam, cover and seal.

making cherry jam with commercial pectin

Fruits with a low pectin content require additional pectin to achieve a good set. Adding commercial pectin is an easy way to do this. Jams made in this way need only short boiling and require little or no water and a smaller proportion of fruit to sugar.

Makes about 1.8kg/4lb

INGREDIENTS

1.2kg/2½lb/6 cups pitted cherries

150ml/¼ pint/⅔ cup water

45ml/3 tbsp lemon juice

1.3kg/3lb/generous 6¾ cups granulated sugar

250ml/8fl oz/1 cup liquid pectin

1 Put the cherries, water and lemon juice in a large pan. Cover and cook for 15 minutes, stirring, until the cherries are tender.

2 Add the sugar to the pan and stir over a low heat until dissolved completely. Bring to the boil and boil rapidly for 1 minute.

3 Stir the liquid pectin into the jam, return to the boil and cook for 1 minute.

4 Remove the pan from the heat and, using a slotted spoon, skim off any froth from the surface. Set the jam aside and leave to stand for 5 minutes.

5 Stir the jam briefly to distribute the fruit evenly, then pot and seal. Use within 6 months.

PECTIN CONTENT OF FRUIT
Although the pectin content of fruits can vary depending on variety, growing conditions and when the fruits were picked, the list below can be used as a good basic guide to the set that will be achieved.

High Apples, blackcurrants, cranberries, damsons, gooseberries, grapefruit, lemons, limes, loganberries, redcurrants, quinces

Medium Apricots (fresh), apples (eating), bilberries, blackberries (early), grapes, greengages, mulberries, peaches, plums, raspberries

Low Bananas, blackberries (late), cherries, elderberries, figs, guavas, japonica, melons, nectarines, pears, pineapples, rhubarb, strawberries

MAKING CONSERVES

These are very similar to jams, but they have a slightly softer set and contain whole or large pieces of fruit. The fruit is first mixed with sugar and sometimes a little liquid, then allowed to stand for several hours or even days. The sugar draws out the juices from the fruit, making it firmer and minimizing the cooking time needed. The fruit should be just ripe and even in size. Not all fruit is suitable for making conserves; tough fruit skins do not soften when sugar is added, so fruits such as gooseberries are no good for making conserves.

making strawberry conserve

This preserve takes several days to make, so be sure to leave plenty of time for preparation.

Makes about 1.3kg/3lb

INGREDIENTS

1.3kg/3lb small or medium strawberries, hulled

1.3kg/3lb/generous 6¾ cups granulated sugar

1 Layer the hulled strawberries in a large bowl with the sugar. Cover with clear film (plastic wrap) and chill for 24 hours.

2 Transfer the strawberries, sugar and juices to a large heavy pan. Heat gently, stirring occasionally, until the sugar has dissolved. Bring to the boil and cook steadily (not rapidly) for 5 minutes.

3 Leave the mixture to cool, then place in a bowl, cover with clear film and chill for 2 days.

4 Pour the strawberry mixture into a large pan, bring to the boil and cook steadily for 10 minutes, then remove from the heat and set aside for 10 minutes. Stir, then ladle into warmed sterilized jars and seal.

flavouring conserves

Conserves are more luxurious than jams and often include dried fruit, nuts and spirits or liqueurs. These extra ingredients should be added after setting point is reached.

When adding dried fruit or nuts, chop them evenly and allow about 50g/2oz/½ cup fruit or nuts per 750g/1⅔lb conserve.

Choose spirits or liqueurs that complement the flavour of the chosen fruit. For example, add apricot brandy or amaretto liqueur to apricot conserve, kirsch to cherry conserve and ginger wine to melon conserve; allow 30ml/2 tbsp to every 750g/1⅔lb conserve.

TOP TIPS FOR SUCCESSFUL JAM-MAKING

• Always use the freshest fruit possible and avoid overripe fruit.

• If you wash the fruit, dry it well and use promptly because it will deteriorate on standing.

• Cook the fruit very slowly at first over a low heat to extract the maximum amount of juice and pectin. Stir the fruit frequently until very tender, but do not overcook. (Fruit skins toughen once sugar is added.)

• Warm the sugar in a low oven for about 10 minutes before adding it to the fruit. This will help it to dissolve.

• Stir the preserve to ensure the sugar is completely dissolved before boiling.

• Do not stir frequently when boiling. This lowers the temperature and delays reaching setting point.

• It is wasteful to remove scum too often. To help prevent scum from forming, add a small amount of unsalted (sweet) butter (about 15g/½oz/1 tbsp for every 450g/1lb fruit) when you add the sugar.

• Do not move freshly potted preserves until they are cool and have set completely.

MAKING JELLIES

Jellies are made using the juice strained from simmered fruit, which is then boiled with sugar to setting point. There is very little preparation of fruit, other than giving it a quick rinse and roughly chopping larger fruit, but you do need to allow plenty of time to make the jelly itself. The secret to a beautifully clear jelly lies in straining the fruit pulp through a jelly bag, drip by drip, which takes several hours.

The basic principles of jelly-making are the same as those for jam and the same three substances – pectin, sugar and acid – are needed for the jelly to set. A perfectly set jelly should retain its shape and quiver when spooned out of the jar. Fruits that are low in pectin such as strawberries, cherries and pears are not suitable on their own for making jellies, so are usually combined with high-pectin fruit.

Because the fruit pulp is discarded in jelly-making, the yield is not as large as in jam-making. For this reason many jelly recipes have evolved to make the most of wild fruits, which are free, or gluts of home-grown fruit.

Jellies can be served both as sweet and savoury preserves. Some, such as redcurrant, rowan and cranberry jellies, are classic accompaniments for hot or cold roasted meat or game, or are added to gravy for flavour and give an attractive glossy finish. Savoury jellies often contain chopped herbs and sometimes wine vinegar or cider vinegar to give them a sharper flavour. Sweet jellies may be eaten as a spread.

yield of jelly

The final yield of jelly depends on how juicy the fruit is, and this can vary depending on the time of the year, the weather during growth and its ripeness when harvested. Because of this, the juice, rather than the fruit, is measured and the amount of sugar is calculated accordingly. As a general rule, 450g/1lb/2¼ cups sugar is added for each 600ml/1 pint/2½ cups juice. (If the fruit is very rich in pectin, the recipe may suggest adding slightly less sugar.) As a rough guide, recipes containing 450g/1lb/2¼ cups sugar will make about 675–800g/1½–1¾lb jelly.

making redcurrant jelly

Makes about 1.3kg/3lb

INGREDIENTS

1.3kg/3lb just-ripe redcurrants

600ml/1 pint/2½ cups water

about 900g/2lb/4½ cups preserving
  or granulated sugar

1 Check the fruit is clean. If necessary, rinse in cold water and use a little less water in the recipe.

2 Remove the currants from the stalks. There is no need to top and tail the fruit.

3 Place the redcurrants in a large heavy pan with the water and simmer gently for about 30 minutes, or until the fruit is very soft and pulpy. Stir occasionally during cooking to prevent the fruit from catching and burning.

4 Pour the cooked fruit and juices into a sterilized jelly bag suspended over a large bowl. Leave to drain for about 4 hours, or until the juice stops dripping. (Do not press or squeeze the fruit in the bag because this will result in a cloudy jelly.)

5 Discard the pulp remaining in the bag (unless you plan to boil the pulp a second time – see page 34). Pour the juice into the cleaned pan and add 450g/1lb/2¼ cups warmed sugar for each 600ml/1 pint/2½ cups of juice. (When making jellies with low-pectin fruit, stir in a little lemon juice or vinegar to improve the set. This will also help to offset the sweetness of the jelly.)

6 Heat the mixture gently, stirring frequently, until the sugar has completely dissolved, then increase the heat and bring to the boil.

7 Boil the jelly rapidly for about 10 minutes, or until setting point is reached. You can check this using the flake test or wrinkle test, or you can use a jam thermometer. The jelly should be heated to 105°C/220°F.

8 Remove the pan from the heat, then skim any froth from the surface of the jelly using a slotted spoon.

9 Carefully remove the last traces of froth using a piece of kitchen paper. Pot the jelly immediately because it will start to set fairly quickly.

10 Cover and seal the jelly while it is hot, then leave to cool completely. (Do not move or tilt the jars until the jelly is completely cold and set.) Label the jars and store in a cool, dark place.

USING A JELLY BAG

Jelly bags, which are made from heavy-duty calico, cotton flannel or close-weave nylon, allow only the juice from the fruit to flow through, leaving the skins, pulp and pips (seeds) inside the bag. The fruit pulp and juices are very heavy, so strong tape or loops are positioned on the corners for hanging the bag securely on a stand, upturned stool or chair.

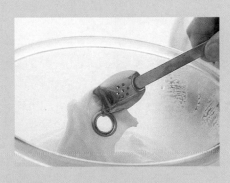

1 Before use, sterilize the jelly bag by scalding in boiling water. This process also helps the juices to run through the bag, rather than being absorbed into it.

2 If you don't have a jelly bag, you can use three or four layers of sterilized muslin (cheesecloth) or a piece of fine linen cloth instead. Simply line a large nylon or stainless-steel sieve (strainer) with the muslin or linen.

3 Carefully suspend the jelly bag or lined sieve over a large bowl to catch the juice. Make sure the bag or sieve is secure before spooning some of the simmered fruit and juices into it. (Don't add too much to start with.)

4 Leave the fruit to drain for a while, then spoon in more fruit. Continue gradually adding fruit in this way until it has all been placed in the bag or sieve, then leave to drain until it stops dripping completely. Some fruits will take 2–3 hours to release all their juice, while others may take as long as 12 hours.

5 Immediately after use, wash the jelly bag thoroughly, then rinse several times to remove all traces of detergent. Ensure the bag is completely dry before storing. The jelly bag may be reused many times, but be sure to sterilize it before every use.

7 To check that the peel is cooked, remove a piece from the pan and leave for a few minutes to cool. Once cooled, press the peel between finger and thumb; it should feel very soft.

8 Using a slotted spoon, remove the muslin bag from the pan and set it aside until cool enough to handle. Squeeze as much liquid as possible back into the pan to extract all the pectin from the pips and pith.

9 Add the sugar to the pan and stir over a low heat until the sugar has completely dissolved.

10 Bring the marmalade to the boil, then boil rapidly for about 10 minutes until setting point is reached (105°C/220°F). You may also use the flake or wrinkle test to check the set.

11 Using a slotted spoon, remove any scum from the surface of the marmalade, then leave to cool until a thin skin starts to form on the surface of the preserve.

12 Leave the marmalade to stand for about 5 minutes, then stir gently to distribute the peel evenly. Ladle into hot sterilized jars, then cover and seal.

making orange jelly marmalade

This recipe uses Seville oranges, and may be made as a plain jelly marmalade, or a few fine shreds of peel can be added before potting, which can look very pretty and adds an interesting texture. Any marmalade can be made in the same way; use exactly the same ingredients listed in the recipe but use the method below.

Makes about 2kg/4½lb

INGREDIENTS

450g/1lb Seville (Temple) oranges

1.75 litres/3 pints/7½ cups water

1.3kg/3lb/generous 6¾ cups preserving or granulated sugar

60ml/4 tbsp lemon juice

1 Wash and dry the oranges; gently scrub them with a soft brush if they have waxed skins.

2 If you want to add a little peel to the jelly marmalade, thinly pare and finely shred the rind from 2 or 3 of the oranges. Place the shreds in a square of muslin (cheesecloth) and tie it into a neat bag.

3 Halve the oranges and squeeze out the juice and pips (seeds), then pour the juice and pips into a large preserving pan.

4 Roughly chop the orange peel, including all the pith, and add it to the pan. Add the bag of shredded rind, if using, and pour over the water. Cover the pan with a lid and leave to soak for at least 4 hours, or overnight.

5 Bring the mixture to the boil, then reduce the heat and simmer gently for 1½ hours. Using a slotted spoon, remove the bag of peel, and carefully remove a piece of peel to check that it is tender. If not, re-tie the bag and simmer for a further 15–20 minutes. Remove the bag of peel and set aside.

6 Line a large nylon or stainless steel sieve (strainer) with a double layer of muslin and place over a large bowl. Pour boiling water through the muslin to scald it. Discard the scalding water. Alternatively, use a scalded jelly bag suspended over a bowl instead of the muslin-lined sieve.

7 Pour the fruit and juices into the sieve or jelly bag and leave to drain for at least 1 hour. Pour the juices into the cleaned pan.

8 Add the sugar, lemon juice and shredded orange rind, if using, to the pan. Stir over a low heat until the sugar has dissolved, then bring to the boil and boil rapidly for about 10 minutes until setting point is reached (105°C/220°F).

9 Remove any scum from the surface. Leave to cool until a thin skin starts to form on the surface. Stir, then pot, cover and seal.

TOP TIPS FOR SUCCESSFUL MARMALADE-MAKING

• Always wash citrus fruit well. Most citrus fruits have a wax coating that helps to prolong the life of the fruit, which should be removed before making the fruit into marmalade. Alternatively, buy unwaxed fruit, but always rinse before use.

• When shredding peel, always slice it slightly thinner than required in the finished preserve because the rind will swell slightly during cooking.

• Coarse-cut peel will take longer to soften than finely shredded peel. To reduce cooking time, soak the peel for a few hours in the water and juices before cooking.

• If the fruit needs to be peeled, put it in a bowl of boiling water and leave to stand for a couple of minutes. This will help to loosen the skins and make peeling easier. The rind's flavour will leach into the water, so use the soaking water in place of some of the measured water.

• If using small, thin-skinned fruit such as limes, cut the fruit into quarters lengthways, then slice flesh and rind into thin or thick shreds. If using larger, thick-skinned fruit such as grapefruit, pare off the peel, including some white pith, and shred. Cut the fruit into quarters, remove the remaining white pith and roughly chop the flesh.

• To make a coarse-cut preserve, boil the whole fruit for 2 hours until soft; pierce with a skewer to test. Lift out the fruit, halve, prise out the pips, then tie them loosely in muslin (cheesecloth) and add to the hot water. Boil rapidly for 10 minutes, then remove the bag. Slice the fruit and return to the pan. Stir in the sugar until dissolved, then boil to setting point.

• Shredded peel should be simmered gently; fierce cooking can give a tough result. Check that the peel is really soft before adding the sugar because it will not tenderize further after this.

• For easy removal, tie the muslin bag of pith and pips with string and attach it to the pan handle. It can then be lifted out of the boiling mixture easily.

• If the fruit contains a lot of pith, put only a small amount in the muslin bag with the pips. Put the remaining pith in a small pan, cover with water and boil for 10 minutes. Strain the liquid and use in place of some of the measured water for the recipe.

• To flavour marmalade with liqueur or spirits, add 15–30ml/ 1–2 tbsp for every 450g/1lb/ 2¼ cups sugar – stir it in just before potting. Unsweetened apple juice or dry (hard) cider may be used to replace up to half the water to add flavour to marmalades made with sharper fruits such as kumquats.

MAKING FRUIT CURDS, BUTTERS AND CHEESES

These rich, creamy preserves were once the highlight of an English tea during Edwardian and Victorian times. Curds and butters are delicious spread on slices of fresh bread and butter, or used as fillings for cakes; firmer fruit cheeses are usually sliced and can be enjoyed in similar ways. Fruit cheeses and butters are also very good served with roast meat, game or cheese.

Curds are made from fruit juice or purée cooked with eggs and butter. They have a soft texture and short keeping qualities. Fruit butters and cheeses are made from fruit purée boiled with sugar and are good if you have a glut of fruit because they require a relatively high proportion of fruit. Butters are lower in sugar and cooked for a shorter time, producing a soft, fruity preserve with a short shelf-life. Cheeses have a firm texture and may be set in moulds and turned out to serve.

MAKING FRUIT CURDS

Fruit curds are usually made with the juice of citrus fruits, but other acidic fruits such as passion fruit may be used. Smooth purées made from, for example, cooking apples or gooseberries can also be used.

The juice or purée is heated with eggs, butter and sugar until thick. The mixture is always cooked in a double boiler or a bowl set over a pan of simmering water to prevent the eggs curdling. Whole eggs are generally used, but if there is a lot of juice, egg yolks or a combination of whole eggs and yolks give a thicker result.

making lime curd

Makes about 675g/1½lb

INGREDIENTS

5 large, ripe juicy limes

115g/4oz/½ cup butter, cubed, at room temperature

350g/12oz/scant 1¾ cups caster (superfine) sugar

4 eggs, at room temperature

1 Finely grate the lime rind, ensuring you do not include any of the bitter white pith. Halve the limes and squeeze out the juice.

2 Place the lime rind in a large heatproof bowl set over a pan of barely simmering water, then strain in the lime juice to remove any bits of fruit or pips (seeds).

3 Add the cubed butter and the sugar to the bowl. Heat gently, stirring frequently, until the butter melts; the mixture should be barely warm, not hot.

4 Lightly beat the eggs with a fork, then strain through a fine sieve into the warm fruit mixture.

5 Keeping the water at a very gentle simmer, stir the fruit mixture continuously until the curd is thick enough to coat the back of a wooden spoon. Do not overcook because the curd will thicken on cooling.

6 Spoon the curd into warmed sterilized jars, then cover and seal when cold. Store in a cool, dark place, ideally in the refrigerator. Use within 2 months.

MAKING FRUIT BUTTERS

Smoother and thicker than jam, fruit butters have a spreadable quality not unlike dairy butter. Many recipes also contain a small amount of butter.

making apricot butter

Makes about 1.3kg/3lb

INGREDIENTS

1.3kg/3lb fresh ripe apricots

1 large orange

about 450ml/¾ pint/scant 2 cups water

about 675g/1½lb/scant 3½ cups caster (superfine) sugar

15g/½oz/1 tbsp butter (optional)

1 Rinse the apricots, then halve, stone (pit) and roughly chop. Remove the skins, unless you are going to purée the fruit by pressing through a sieve (strainer).

2 Scrub the orange and thinly pare 2–3 large strips of rind, avoiding any pith. Squeeze out the juice and put the apricots and the orange rind and juice in a large heavy pan.

3 Pour over enough of the water to cover the fruit. Bring to the boil, half-cover, then reduce the heat and simmer for 45 minutes.

4 Remove the orange rind, then blend the apricot mixture in a food processor until very smooth. Alternatively, press through a fine nylon or stainless steel sieve.

5 Measure the apricot purée and return it to the cleaned pan, adding 375g/13oz/1¾ cups sugar for each 600ml/1 pint/2½ cups purée.

6 Heat the mixture gently, stirring, until the sugar has dissolved, then bring to the boil and boil for about 20 minutes, stirring frequently, until thick and creamy. Remove the pan from the heat.

7 If using, stir the butter into the mixture until melted. (The butter gives a glossy finish.) Spoon into warmed sterilized jars and cover. Store in the refrigerator and use within 6 months.

MAKING FRUIT CHEESES

These sweet, firm preserves are known as cheeses because they are stiff enough to be cut into slices or wedges rather like their dairy counterparts. This name is particularly appropriate when the cheeses are set in moulds and turned out. They may be made either from fresh fruit, or from the pulp left from making jellies.

making cranberry and apple cheese

Makes about 900g/2lb

INGREDIENTS

450g/1lb/4 cups fresh cranberries
225g/8oz cooking apples
600ml/1 pint/2½ cups water
10ml/2 tsp lemon juice
about 450g/1lb/2¼ cups
  granulated sugar
glycerine, for greasing (optional)

1 Rinse the cranberries and place in a large heavy pan. Wash the apples and cut into small pieces (there is no need to peel or core). Add the water and lemon juice.

2 Cover the pan with a lid and bring the mixture to the boil; do not lift the lid until the cranberries stop popping because they often jump out of the pan and can be very hot. Simmer gently for 1 hour, or until the fruit is soft and pulpy.

3 Press the mixture through a fine nylon or stainless steel sieve (strainer) into a bowl.

4 Weigh the purée, then return it to the cleaned pan, adding 450g/1lb/ 2¼ cups sugar for every 450g/1lb purée. Gently heat the mixture over a low heat, stirring, until the sugar has dissolved completely.

5 Increase the heat a little and simmer the mixture until it is so thick that the spoon leaves a clean line through the mixture when drawn across the pan. It may take as long as 30 minutes to reduce the purée to this consistency. Stir frequently to stop the mixture burning on the base of the pan.

6 Spoon the fruit cheese into warmed sterilized jars and seal. Alternatively, spoon the mixture into moulds or jars greased with a little glycerine and cover with clear film (plastic wrap) when cool. In sealed jars, the cheese will keep for up to 1 year; in covered moulds, it should be kept in the refrigerator until you are ready to turn it out; eat within 1 month of making.

USING LEFTOVER PULP

The fruit pulp left from jelly-making is perfect for making into fruit cheeses. Remove the pulp from the jelly bag, stir in enough hot water to make a soft purée, then push through a sieve (strainer). Place the purée in a clean pan, adding 450g/1lb/2¼ cups sugar for every 450g/1lb purée, and follow the instructions for making fruit cheese above.

MAKING BOTTLED FRUITS

This is a traditional method of preserving fruit in syrup. The jars or bottles of fruit and syrup are heated to destroy micro-organisms. Although superseded by freezing, bottling is more suitable for some fruits such as peaches, pears, grapes and oranges; the method is less suitable for preserving soft berries such as raspberries.

making bottled fresh fruit salad

Makes about 1.8kg/4lb

INGREDIENTS

250g/9oz/generous 1¼ cups
  granulated sugar

350ml/12fl oz/1½ cups water

1 lemon

450g/1lb each eating apples, pears,
  and peaches or nectarines

350g/12oz seedless green grapes

4 oranges

1 Put the sugar and water in a pan. Pare off a small strip of lemon rind, avoiding the pith, and add to the pan. Heat gently, stirring, until the sugar has dissolved. Bring to the boil and simmer for 1 minute. Cover and leave to stand.

2 Halve the lemon, then squeeze out the juice and strain.

3 Prepare the fruit, allowing 275g/10oz fruit for each 450g/1lb jar. Peel, core and slice the apples and pears and toss in lemon juice. Peel, halve, stone (pit) and slice the peaches or nectarines; halve the grapes; and segment the oranges.

4 Rinse hot sterilized jars with boiling water. Pack the fruit into the jars tightly, pressing down gently with a wooden spoon.

5 Strain the syrup through a fine sieve and return it to the cleaned pan. Bring to the boil, then pour over the fruit, filling the jars to within 1cm/½in of the top. Cover and heat-treat.

making poached pears

Fruit is often poached in syrup until just tender before bottling.

Makes about 1.8kg/4lb

INGREDIENTS

225g/8oz/scant 1¼ cups
  granulated sugar

1.2 litres/2 pints/5 cups water

1 orange

1 cinnamon stick

2kg/4½ lb cooking pears

1 Put the sugar and water in a large, wide pan and add a thinly pared strip of orange rind and the cinnamon. Heat gently until the sugar has dissolved, then bring to the boil and simmer for 1 minute.

2 Squeeze the juice from the orange, then strain. Peel and core the pears, then toss in lemon juice as soon as each one is prepared.

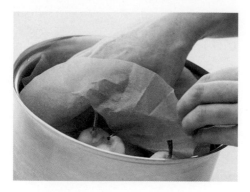

3 Add the pears to the syrup in a single layer. Place greaseproof (waxed) paper over the pears to keep them immersed. Poach for 15 minutes until just tender and slightly translucent; the syrup should hardly bubble so that the fruit holds its shape. Once cooked, bottle and heat-treat.

MAKING SUGAR SYRUPS

Poach whole and slightly hard fruits such as pears and plums in a light syrup; poach figs, peaches, nectarines and apricots in a medium syrup; and poach soft fruits such as strawberries and raspberries in a heavy syrup.

To make a light syrup, use 115g/4oz/generous ½ cup sugar to 600ml/1 pint/2½ cups water; to make a medium syrup, use 175g/6oz/scant 1 cup sugar to 600ml/1 pint/2½ cups water; to make a heavy syrup, use 350g/12oz/1¾ cups sugar to 600ml/1 pint/2½ cups water.

Put the sugar and water in a pan and heat gently, stirring, until the sugar has dissolved. Bring to the boil and simmer for 1 minute. Use hot or cool.

HEAT TREATMENT

There are several ways to heat-treat bottled fruit. The filled jars may be heated in hot water, in the oven, or in a pressure cooker. As the fruit cools, a vacuum is created.

Use jars specifically designed for heat treatment. Preserving jars with clamp tops should be sealed once filled; the clamps expand slightly to allow steam to escape. Screw tops on preserving jars should not be tightened until after heating because the steam will not be able to escape and the jars may burst. Heat-treated preserves may be kept for up to 2 years.

water bath method

This is suitable for fruits bottled in either hot or cold syrup; the latter will take a little longer to process.

1 Wrap folded newspaper or cloth around each filled container, then stand them on a metal trivet or a thick layer of paper or cloth in a large heavy pan. (Containers placed directly on the pan may crack.)

2 Pour tepid water around the jars, right up to the neck, then cover the pan. Bring slowly to the boil (this should take 25–30 minutes), then simmer for the required time.

3 Turn off the heat and ladle out some of the hot water. Using tongs or oven gloves, lift the containers out of the pan and place on a wooden board. If they have screw-band lids, tighten immediately.

4 Leave the containers to cool for 24 hours, then remove the screw bands or clips. Holding the rim of the lid, carefully lift the container; it should hold its own weight. Containers with one-piece lids should have a very slight dip in the lid to indicate that they are sealed. If a jar is not sealed properly, it should be stored in the refrigerator and used as soon as possible.

HEATING TIMES FOR THE WATER BATH METHOD
The following times are for fruit packed in hot syrup after boiling. Allow 5 minutes more for fruit packed in cold syrup.

Fruit	Minutes
Soft berries and	
redcurrants	2
Blackcurrants,	
gooseberries, rhubarb,	
cherries, apricots	
and plums	10
Peaches and nectarines	20
Figs and pears	35

moderate oven method

This is only suitable for fruits covered with hot syrup; cold-filled jars may crack in the warm oven.

1 Preheat the oven to 150°C/300°F/Gas 2. Put the rubber rings and lids on the filled jars, but do not seal. Place in a roasting pan lined with newspaper or cloth, spacing the jars about 5cm/2in apart. Pour 1cm/½in boiling water into the pan.

2 Place the pan in the middle of the oven. Cook 500–600ml/17–20fl oz jars for 30–35 minutes and 1 litre/1¾ pint jars for 35–55 minutes. If there are more than four jars, allow a little extra time.

3 Remove from the oven and seal the lids immediately. Cool on a wooden board. Test the seals as for the water bath method.

pressure cooker method

If using clip-top jars, move the clips slightly to the side of the lid to reduce the pressure. Check the instructions for the pressure cooker.

1 Stand the jars on the trivet in the pressure cooker, ensuring they do not touch each other or the pan.

2 Pour in 600ml/1 pint/2½ cups hot water. Put on the lid with a low (2.25kg/5lb) weight and slowly bring to pressure. Maintain this pressure for 4 minutes. Leave to stand until the pressure drops.

3 Transfer the jars to a board and seal. Leave for 12 hours, then test as for the water bath method.

MAKING CANDIED AND GLACÉ FRUIT

Sugar is an excellent preservative. Candying is a method by which fruit or citrus peel is preserved by steeping in syrup. The fruit or peel becomes so saturated in sugar that natural deterioration is virtually halted. The process works by gradually replacing the fruit's moisture with a saturated sugar solution. This has to be done slowly and takes at least 15 days, but is well worth it. Candied fruit is expensive to buy and, although you need to plan ahead when making candied fruit or peel, it requires only a little time each day.

making candied fruit

You can candy as much or as little fruit as you like, working with the basic proportions of fruit to sugar given in the recipe below. Always candy different fruits separately, so that each type retains its own flavour. Choose firm, fresh fruits that are free of blemishes.

INGREDIENTS

fresh, firm, just-ripe fruit, such as
  pineapples, peaches, pears, apples,
  plums, apricots, kiwi fruit or cherries
granulated sugar
caster (superfine) sugar, for sprinkling

Day 1

1 Prepare the fruit. Thickly peel and core pineapples, then slice into rings; peel, stone (pit) or core peaches, pears and apples, then halve or cut into thick slices; plums and apricots can be left whole (prick them all over with a fine skewer) or halve and stone; skin and quarter kiwi fruits, or thickly slice; stone cherries.

2 Weigh the fruit, then put in a pan and just cover with water. Bring to the boil and simmer until just tender. Do not overcook because the flavour and shape will be lost; do not undercook because the fruit will be tough when candied.

3 Using a slotted spoon, lift the cooked fruit into a large wide bowl; avoid piling the fruit up high. Retain the cooking liquid.

4 For every 450g/1lb prepared (uncooked) fruit, use 300ml/½ pint/ 1¼ cups of the cooking liquid and 175g/6oz/scant 1 cup sugar. Gently heat the sugar and liquid in a pan, stirring, until the sugar has dissolved, then bring to the boil.

5 Pour the boiling syrup over the fruit, making sure that the fruit is completely immersed. Cover and leave to stand for 24 hours.

Day 2

1 Drain the syrup from the fruit back into a pan, being careful not to damage the fruit as you do so. Return the fruit to the bowl.

2 Add 50g/2oz/¼ cup granulated sugar to the syrup and heat gently, stirring until dissolved completely, then bring to the boil.

3 Pour the hot syrup over the fruit. Allow to cool, then cover and leave to stand for 24 hours.

Days 3–7

Repeat the instructions for day 2 every day for the next 5 days. The concentration of sugar will become much stronger.

Days 8–9

1 Drain the syrup from the fruit into a large wide pan and add 90g/3½oz/½ cup sugar. Heat gently, stirring, until dissolved.

2 Carefully add the fruit to the syrup and simmer gently for about 3 minutes. Return the fruit and syrup to the bowl, cool, then cover and leave to stand for 48 hours.

Days 10–13

Repeat the instructions for days 8–9, leaving the fruit to soak for 4 days rather than 2.

COOK'S TIP

The final soaking stage from days 10–13 can be extended another 6 days, if you like – to a total of 10 days. The longer the fruit is left to soak in the syrup, the sweeter and more intense its flavour will become.

Days 14–15

1 Drain the fruit, discarding the syrup. Carefully spread the fruit out, spacing each piece slightly apart, on a wire rack placed over a baking sheet.

2 Cut a sheet of baking parchment or foil slightly larger than the baking sheet. Using a fine skewer, prick about 12 tiny holes at equal intervals in the sheet.

3 Cover the fruit with the baking parchment or foil, being very careful not to touch the fruit. The parchment or foil is simply to keep off any dust; some air should still be able to circulate around the fruit.

4 Leave the fruit in a warm place such as a sunny windowsill or airing cupboard for 2 days, turning each piece of fruit occasionally until all the fruit is thoroughly dry.

5 Sprinkle the fruit with a little caster sugar, then store in an airtight container in single layers between sheets of greaseproof (waxed) paper. Eat within 1 year.

COOK'S TIP

Candied fruits are very pretty, retaining the colour of the original fruits. They make great sweetmeats for serving after a meal, particularly at Christmas.

making candied peel

Citrus peel contains less moisture than the fruit, making candying simpler and less time-consuming.

INGREDIENTS

5 small oranges, 6 lemons or 7 limes, or a combination

granulated sugar

caster (superfine) sugar, for sprinkling

1 Scrub the fruit. Remove the peel in quarters, scraping away the pith. Place in a pan, cover with cold water and simmer for 1¼–1½ hours. Drain, reserving 300ml/½ pint/ 1¼ cups of the cooking water.

2 Pour the reserved water into the pan and add 200g/7oz/1 cup sugar. Heat gently, stirring until dissolved, then bring to the boil. Add the peel and simmer for 1 minute. Leave to cool, tip into a bowl, cover and leave for 48 hours.

3 Remove the peel and pour the syrup back into the pan. Add 150g/ 5oz/¾ cup sugar and heat gently, stirring until dissolved. Add the peel, bring to the boil, then simmer until transparent. Cool, pour into a bowl, cover and leave for 2 weeks.

4 Drain the peel, then dry, sprinkle and store in the same way as candied fruit.

making glacé fruit

Glacé, or crystallized, fruit is made from candied fruit, dipped in heavy syrup to give it a glossy coating.

INGREDIENTS

candied fruit

400g/14oz/2 cups granulated sugar

120ml/4fl oz/½ cup water

1 Make sure the candied fruit is dry and dust off any sugar coating. Put the sugar and water in a pan and heat gently, stirring, until the sugar has completely dissolved. Bring to the boil and simmer for 2 minutes.

2 Pour one-third of the syrup into a small bowl. Fill a second bowl with boiling water. Using a slotted spoon or fork, first dip the fruit into the boiling water for 15 seconds, then shake and dip into the syrup for 15 seconds. Place on a wire rack.

3 Repeat with the remaining fruit, topping up the bowl of syrup when necessary (return the syrup to the boil before doing this); replace the bowl of boiling water once or twice.

4 Dry the fruit on wire racks placed over baking sheets in a very warm place for 2–3 days, turning the fruit occasionally. Store in the same way as candied fruit.

MAKING DRIED FRUITS AND VEGETABLES

Removing moisture from foods is one of the oldest methods of preserving. Traditional techniques depend on the correct proportions of sunlight, heat and humidity for successful results. If food is dried too fast, moisture can get trapped and spoil it; if it is dried too slowly, micro-organisms may start to grow. Most commercially dried fruits and vegetables, such as apricots, figs and tomatoes, which are high both in sugar and acid, are still wind- and sun-dried in the way they have been for centuries.

To re-create these conditions, an airy place with a steady temperature is needed. A very warm room or cupboard may be used if the temperature is constant, but the most efficient way is to use an oven on the lowest setting.

A fan oven is ideal because of the constant circulation of air. If using a conventional oven, leave the door open with the tiniest possible gap, or open frequently during the drying process to let steam escape. Be careful that the temperature does not become too high, or the fruit or vegetables will cook and shrivel. If necessary, turn off the oven occasionally and leave it to cool down.

Choose firm, fresh and ripe fruit and vegetables for drying. Citrus fruits and melons consist mainly of water, so do not dry well, nor do berry fruits because they discolour and become very seedy. To help preserve the dried fruit and prevent discoloration, the prepared pieces should be dipped into a very weak brine solution, or acidulated water, before drying.

making dried apple rings

INGREDIENTS

15ml/1 tbsp salt, or 90ml/6 tbsp lemon juice, or 30ml/2 tbsp ascorbic acid (vitamin C) powder

1.2 litres/2 pints/5 cups water

900g/2lb firm, ripe apples

1 Put the salt, lemon juice or ascorbic acid powder in a large bowl and pour in the water. Stir until dissolved.

2 Peel and core the apples, then cut into rings slightly thicker than 5mm/¼in. As soon as each apple is cut, put the rings in the bowl of water and leave for 1 minute before lifting out. Pat the rings dry using kitchen paper.

3 Thread the apple rings on to wooden skewers, leaving a small space between each ring, or spread the apple rings out on wire racks. (Baking sheets are not suitable because air needs to circulate around the fruit.)

4 If using skewers, rest them on the oven shelves, allowing the apple rings to hang between the gaps. If using wire racks, simply place the racks in the oven. Leave the door very slightly ajar.

5 Dry the apples at 110°C/225°F/ Gas ¼ for about 5 hours, or until the apple rings resemble soft, pliable leather.

6 Remove the fruit from the oven and leave to cool completely. Very crisp fruits and vegetables should be stored in airtight containers, but leathery, pliable fruits are better stored in paper bags or cardboard boxes; storing them in plastic bags may make them go mouldy.

7 To reconstitute the dried apple slices, put them in a bowl and pour over boiling water. Leave to soak for at least 5 minutes, then place in a pan and gently cook in the soaking liquid.

COOK'S TIPS

• Dried apple slices make a healthy snack and are popular with children.

• They are also good chopped and added to desserts and cakes.

PRESERVING FRUITS IN ALCOHOL

Fruits preserved in alcohol make luxurious instant desserts, served with crème fraîche or ice cream. One of the best-known fruit and alcohol preserves is German *rumtopf*, which means rum pot. It consists of summer and early autumn fruits bottled in alcohol, usually rum, but not always, with a little sugar. Traditionally, this preserve is made in a large jar with a wide neck and tight-fitting lid.

Pure alcohol is the best preservative because bacteria and moulds are unable to grow in it. Clear liqueurs, such as eau de vie, orange liqueur, Kirsch and Amaretto, or spirits such as brandy, rum and vodka, which are at least 40% ABV, may be used.

The alcohol content of table wine and cider is too low and so these are not effective preservatives on their own unless the bottles are heat-treated. Fruits preserved in wine or cider should be stored in the refrigerator and used within 1 month of making.

When using alcohol to preserve, it is usually best to combine it with sugar syrup because high-alcohol liqueurs and spirits tend to shrink the fruit. Most fruits are first simmered in syrup, which helps to tenderize the fruit and kills the bad enzymes.

The type of syrup used for preserving fruits in alcohol varies depending on the sweetness and juiciness of the fruit, as well as the desired result. A typical syrup would be 600ml/1 pint/2½ cups alcohol, blended with a syrup of 150ml/¼ pint/⅔ cup water and 150g/5oz/¾ cup sugar.

making nectarines in brandy syrup

For extra flavour, you can add whole spices such as vanilla or cinnamon to the syrup.

Makes about 900g/2lb

INGREDIENTS

350g/12oz/1¾ cups preserving or granulated sugar
150ml/¼ pint/⅔ cup water
450g/1lb firm, ripe nectarines
2 bay leaves
150ml/¼ pint/⅔ cup brandy

1 Put the sugar in a large heavy pan with the water and heat gently, stirring until dissolved completely. Bring to the boil, then reduce the heat and simmer for 10 minutes.

2 Halve and stone (pit) the nectarines. (If liked, you may also peel them.) Add them to the syrup.

3 Reduce the heat so that the syrup is barely simmering and poach the nectarines until almost tender. Add the bay leaves 1 minute before the end of the cooking. Turn off the heat and leave them to stand for 5 minutes; they will cook a little more as it cools.

4 Using a slotted spoon, lift the fruit out of the pan and pack into hot sterilized jars.

5 Bring the syrup to a rapid boil and cook for 3–4 minutes. Leave to cool for a few minutes, then stir in the brandy. (Do not add the brandy to the boiling syrup because the alcohol will evaporate and the syrup will lose its preserving qualities.) Pour the syrup into the jars, covering the fruit completely. Tap the jars to release any air and seal. Store in a cool dark place and use within 1 year.

MODERN PRESERVING TECHNIQUES

With the advent of new kitchen equipment such as microwaves, pressure cookers and freezers, new ways to make fruit preserves have developed. The increased concern over healthy eating has also led to new types of preserves such as reduced-sugar jams.

PRESERVING IN A MICROWAVE

Preserves can be made using a microwave, but only using specific recipes intended for the appliance. It is difficult to adapt conventional recipes because many rely on the evaporation of liquid to achieve a set or to thicken the preserve.

Make sure the ingredients are at room temperature; if they are not, it will affect cooking times. Frozen fruit can be used to make microwave preserves, but it must be defrosted first.

Chop fruit into equal-size pieces so that they cook at the same speed, and stir the preserve frequently during cooking to distribute the heat evenly and avoid hot spots. Use a suitable microwave-proof bowl that will withstand very hot temperatures, and that is large enough to hold twice the volume of the ingredients.

When the preserve has finished cooking, leave it to stand for several minutes until it has stopped bubbling. It is essential to protect your hands with oven gloves when lifting the bowl; take care not to place it on a cold surface because this may cause the glass to crack – a wooden board is ideal for protecting the surface and bowl.

making microwave lemon curd

This recipe is based on an 800 watt microwave. For microwaves with a different wattage, adjust cooking times as follows – for a 900 watt oven: subtract 10 seconds per minute; for a 850 watt oven: subtract 5 seconds per minute; for a 750 watt oven: add 5 seconds per minute; for a 700 watt oven: add 10 seconds per minute.

Makes about 450g/1lb

INGREDIENTS

115g/4oz/½ cup butter, cubed

finely grated rind and juice of 3 large lemons

225g/8oz/generous 1 cup caster (superfine) sugar

3 eggs plus 1 egg yolk

1 Put the butter, lemon rind and juice in a large microwave-proof bowl. Cook on high for 3 minutes.

2 Add the sugar to the bowl and stir for 1 minute until it has almost dissolved. Return to the microwave and cook on 100% power for 2 minutes, stirring every 1 minute.

3 Beat the eggs and the yolk together, then whisk into the lemon mixture, a little at a time.

4 Cook on 40% power, for 10–12 minutes, whisking every 2 minutes, until the curd thickens. Ladle into hot sterilized jars, cover and seal. When cool, store in the refrigerator. Use within 2 months.

PRESERVING USING A PRESSURE COOKER

Preserves can be made very quickly using a pressure cooker. They are particularly useful for marmalades and for softening whole or hard fruits. Never fill the pan more than half full and always check the manufacturer's instructions.

making pressure-cooker orange marmalade

Makes about 2.5kg/5½lb

INGREDIENTS

900g/2lb Seville (Temple) oranges

1 large lemon

1.2 litres/2 pints/5 cups water

1.8kg/4lb/generous 9 cups preserving or granulated sugar

1 Scrub the fruit, then halve and squeeze out the juice, retaining any pips. Quarter the oranges, scrape off the pulp and membranes and tie in a piece of muslin (cheesecloth) with the lemon halves and any pips.

2 Place the orange peel in the pressure cooker with the muslin bag and 900ml/1½ pints/3¾ cups of the water. Bring to medium (4.5kg/10lb) pressure and cook for 10 minutes.

3 Reduce the pressure and leave until the fruit is cool enough to handle. Remove the muslin bag and squeeze it over the pan.

4 Cut the orange peel into fine shreds and return to the pan with the remaining water and the fruit juice. Add the sugar and heat gently until the sugar has dissolved. Bring to the boil, then boil rapidly for about 10 minutes until setting point is reached (105°C/220°F).

5 Remove any scum from the surface using a slotted spoon, then leave the marmalade to cool until a thin skin starts to form on the surface. Stir gently to distribute the peel evenly, then ladle into hot sterilized jars, cover and seal.

MAKING FREEZER JAMS

This type of jam is not cooked, so it has a fresher, fruitier flavour and a brighter colour than cooked jam. Once thawed, it does not keep as well as traditional jam. Commercial pectin is used as a setting agent.

making strawberry freezer jam

Makes about 1.3kg/3lb

INGREDIENTS
800g/1¾lb/7 cups strawberries
900g/2lb/4½ cups caster (superfine) sugar
30ml/2 tbsp lemon juice
120ml/4fl oz/½ cup commercial liquid pectin

1 Wipe the fruit. (Only wash if necessary, then pat dry on kitchen paper.) Hull and cut into quarters, then put in a bowl with the sugar.

2 Lightly mash the fruit with a fork, leaving plenty of lumps of fruit. Cover and leave to stand for 1 hour, stirring once or twice.

3 Add the lemon juice and pectin to the fruit and stir for 4 minutes until thoroughly combined. Ladle the jam into small freezer-proof containers, cover and leave to stand for about 4 hours.

4 Put the jam in the refrigerator and chill for 24–48 hours, or until the jam sets. Freeze the jam for up to 6 months, or until ready to use.

5 To serve, remove the jam from the freezer and leave at room temperature for about 1 hour, or until defrosted. Keep any leftover defrosted jam in the refrigerator and use quickly.

MAKING REDUCED-SUGAR PRESERVES

Sugar is the vital preserving agent in sweet fruit preserves. It helps to prevent fermentation and spoilage, as well as adding sweetness and flavour, and improving the set. The proportion of sugar required for this is about 60 per cent of the final weight of preserve. Although it is possible to make reduced-sugar preserves, the yield is smaller and they will not keep for as long. In most recipes, the sugar content can be reduced by up to half. The jam should be stored in the refrigerator and used within 4 months.

USING FROZEN FRUIT
Freezing is a quick and convenient way to preserve fruit when it is at its best and cheapest. It is especially useful for fruit with a very short season, such as Seville or Temple oranges. Freezing does destroy some of the pectin content, so to compensate for this, an extra 10 per cent of fruit should be used in the recipe. Do a pectin test during cooking to check the set.

jams and conserves

Preserving fruits in jams and conserves is one of the best ways of enjoying their delicious flavour all year round. In summer, with its long, warm days, there is an abundance of sweet juicy berries, while the autumn harvest offers a fabulous choice of stone and hedgerow fruits. All of these can be made into irresistible jams that can be enjoyed at any time of day – spread on toast, used as a filling or topping for plain cakes, or spooned over ice cream for a treat. All the recipes in this chapter will keep for at least 6 months.

seedless raspberry and passion fruit jam

The pips in raspberry jam can often put people off this wonderful preserve. This version has none of the pips and all of the flavour, and is enhanced by the tangy addition of passion fruit.

Makes about 1.3kg/3lb

INGREDIENTS

1.6kg/3½lb/14 cups raspberries

4 passion fruit, halved

1.3kg/3lb/6½ cups preserving sugar
   with pectin, warmed

juice of 1 lemon

COOK'S TIPS

• Check the instructions on the sugar packet for details of the boiling time.

• If you cannot find preserving sugar with pectin, use the same quantity of regular sugar and add powdered or liquid pectin. Check the instructions on the packet for quantities.

1 Place the raspberries in a large pan, then scoop out the passion fruit seeds and pulp and add to the raspberries. Cover and cook over a low heat for 20 minutes, or until the juices begin to run.

2 Remove the pan from the heat and leave to cool slightly, then, using the back of a spoon, press the fruit through a coarse sieve into a preserving pan.

3 Add the sugar and lemon juice to the pan and stir over a low heat until the sugar has dissolved. Bring to the boil and cook for 4 minutes, or until the jam reaches setting point (105°C/220°F).

4 Remove the pan from the heat and skim off any scum. Leave to cool slightly, then pour into warmed sterilized jars. Seal and label, then store in a cool place.

wild strawberry and rose petal conserve

This fragrant jam is ideal served with summer cream teas. Rose water complements the strawberries beautifully, but only add a few drops because the flavour can easily become over-powering.

Makes about 900g/2lb

INGREDIENTS

000g/2lb/8 cups wild Alpine
  strawberries

450g/1lb/4 cups strawberries, hulled
  and mashed

2 dark pink rose buds, petals only

juice of 2 lemons

1.3kg/3lb/6½ cups granulated
  sugar, warmed

a few drops of rose water

1 Put all the strawberries in a non-metallic bowl with the rose petals, lemon juice and warmed sugar. Cover and leave overnight.

2 The next day, tip the fruit into a preserving pan and heat gently, stirring, until all the sugar has dissolved. Boil for 10–15 minutes, or to setting point (105°C/220°F).

3 Stir the rose water into the jam, then remove the pan from the heat. Skim off any scum and leave to cool for 5 minutes, then stir and pour into warmed sterilized jars. Seal and label, then store.

COOK'S TIPS

• If you are unable to find wild berries, use ordinary strawberries instead. Leave the smaller berries whole but mash any large ones.

• To make plain strawberry jam, make in the same way but leave out the rose petals and rose water.

cherry-berry conserve

Tart cranberries enliven the taste of cherries and also add an essential dose of pectin to this pretty conserve, which is fabulous spread on crumpets or toast. It is also delicious stirred into meaty gravies and sauces served with roast duck, poultry or pork.

2 Add the water to the pan. Cover and bring to the boil, then simmer for 20–30 minutes, or until the cranberries are very tender.

3 Add the sugar to the pan and heat gently, stirring, until the sugar has dissolved. Bring to the boil, then cook for 10 minutes, or to setting point (105°C/220°F).

4 Remove the pan from the heat and skim off any scum using a slotted spoon. Leave to cool for 10 minutes, then stir gently and pour into warmed sterilized jars. Seal, label and store.

Makes about 1.3kg/3lb

INGREDIENTS

350g/12oz/3 cups fresh cranberries

1kg/2¼lb/5½ cups cherries, pitted

120ml/4fl oz/½ cup blackcurrant or raspberry syrup

juice of 2 lemons

250ml/8fl oz/1 cup water

1.3kg/3lb/6½ cups preserving or granulated sugar, warmed

COOK'S TIP

The cranberries must be cooked until very tender before the sugar is added, otherwise they will become tough.

1 Put the cranberries in a food processor and process until coarsely chopped. Scrape into a pan and add the cherries, fruit syrup and lemon juice.

summer berry and juniper jam

In late summer, there is a moment when all the different varieties of berries suddenly seem to be ripe at the same time. Combine them in jam as the flavours work well together, particularly when blended with juniper, which produces a taste reminiscent of gin.

Makes about 1.3kg/3lb

INGREDIENTS

675g/1½lb/6 cups raspberries

675g/1½lb/6 cups blackberries

10ml/2 tsp juniper berries, crushed

300ml/½ pint/1¼ cups water

1.3kg/3lb/6½ cups granulated sugar, warmed

juice of 2 lemons

COOK'S TIP

Juniper berries are quite soft and are easily broken down into coarsely crushed pieces. Put the berries in a mortar and crush with a pestle.

1 Put the raspberries, blackberries and juniper berries in a large heavy pan with the water. Set over a low heat, cover and cook gently for about 15 minutes, or until the juices begin run.

2 Add the sugar and lemon juice to the pan and cook over a low heat, stirring frequently, until the sugar has dissolved. (Be careful not to break up the berries too much.)

3 Bring to the boil and cook for 5–10 minutes, or until the jam reaches setting point (105°C/220°F). Remove the pan from the heat and skim off any scum from the surface using a slotted spoon. Leave to cool for about 5 minutes, then stir gently and pour into warmed sterilized jars. Seal and label, then store in a cool, dark place.

blueberry and lime jam

The subtle yet fragrant flavour of blueberries can be elusive on its own. Adding a generous quantity of tangy lime juice enhances their flavour and gives this jam a wonderful zesty taste.

Makes about 1.3kg/3lb

INGREDIENTS

1.3kg/3lb/12 cups blueberries

finely pared rind and juice
  of 4 limes

1kg/2¼lb/5 cups preserving sugar
  with pectin

COOK'S TIP

Blueberries are not naturally high in pectin, so extra pectin is needed for a good set. If you prefer, used granulated sugar and add pectin according to the instruction on the packet in place of the preserving sugar with pectin.

1 Put the blueberries, lime juice and half the sugar in a large, non-metallic bowl and lightly crush the berries using a potato masher. Set aside for about 4 hours.

2 Tip the crushed berry mixture into a pan and stir in the finely pared lime rind and the remaining preserving sugar. Heat slowly, stirring continuously, until the sugar has completely dissolved.

3 Increase the heat and bring to the boil. Boil rapidly for about 4 minutes, or until the jam reaches setting point (105°C/220°F).

4 Remove the pan from the heat and set aside for 5 minutes. Stir the jam gently, then pour into warmed sterilized jars. Seal the jars, then label when completely cool. Store in a cool, dark place.

blackcurrant jam

This jam has a rich, fruity flavour and a wonderfully strong dark colour. It is punchy and delicious with scones for tea or spread on croissants for a continental-style breakfast.

Makes about 1.3kg/3lb

INGREDIENTS

1.3kg/3lb/12 cups blackcurrants
grated rind and juice of 1 orange
475ml/16fl oz/2 cups water
1.3kg/3lb/6½ cups granulated
  sugar, warmed
30ml/2 tbsp cassis (optional)

1 Place the blackcurrants, orange rind and juice and water in a large heavy pan. Bring to the boil, reduce the heat and simmer for 30 minutes.

2 Add the warmed sugar to the pan and stir over a low heat until the sugar has dissolved.

3 Bring the mixture to the boil and cook for about 8 minutes, or until the jam reaches setting point (105°C/220°F).

4 Remove the pan from the heat and skim off any scum from the surface using a slotted spoon. Leave to cool for 5 minutes, then stir in the cassis, if using.

5 Pour the jam into warmed sterilized jars and seal. Leave the jars to cool completely, then label and store in a cool, dark place.

dried apricot jam

This richly flavoured jam can be made at any time of year, so even if you miss the short apricot season, you can still enjoy the delicious taste of sweet, tangy apricot jam all year round.

Makes about 2kg/4½lb

INGREDIENTS

675g/1½lb dried apricots

900ml/1½ pints/3¾ cups apple juice

juice and grated rind of
2 unwaxed lemons

675g/1½lb/scant 3½ cups preserving
or granulated sugar, warmed

50g/2oz/½ cup blanched almonds,
coarsely chopped

COOK'S TIP

Use the best quality traditional dried apricots to make this jam. They have a more suitable texture than the soft ready-to-eat dried apricots and will produce a better end result.

1 Put the apricots in a bowl, pour over the apple juice and leave to soak overnight.

2 Pour the soaked apricots and juice into a preserving pan and add the lemon juice and rind. Bring to the boil, then lower the heat and simmer for 15–20 minutes until the apricots are soft.

3 Add the warmed sugar to the pan and bring to the boil, stirring until the sugar has completely dissolved. Boil for 15–20 minutes, or until setting point is reached (105°C/220°F).

4 Stir the chopped almonds into the jam and leave to stand for about 15 minutes, then pour the jam into warmed, sterilized jars. Seal, then leave to cool completely before labelling. Store in a cool, dark place.

peach and amaretto jam

Adding amaretto (almond liqueur) produces a luxurious jam that's perfect served on warm buttered toast or English muffins. You can use peach schnapps in place of the amaretto if you prefer.

Makes about 1.3kg/3lb

INGREDIENTS

1.3kg/3lb peaches

250ml/8fl oz/1 cup water

juice of 2 lemons

1.3kg/3lb/6½ cups granulated
  sugar, warmed

45ml/3 tbsp amaretto liqueur

1 Carefully peel the peaches using a vegetable peeler, or blanch briefly in boiling water, then peel with a knife. Reserve the skins.

2 Halve and stone (pit) the fruit, dice the flesh and put in a pan with the water. Place the skins in a small pan with water to cover. Boil until the liquid is reduced to 30ml/2 tbsp. Press the skins and liquid through a sieve into the peaches. Cover and simmer for 20 minutes, or until soft.

3 Add the lemon juice and sugar to the pan. Heat, stirring, until the sugar has dissolved completely. Bring to the boil and cook for 10–15 minutes, or to setting point (105°C/220°F). Remove from the heat and skim off any scum from the surface using a slotted spoon.

4 Leave the jam to cool for about 10 minutes, then stir in the amaretto and pour into warmed sterilized jars. Seal, then leave to cool completely before labelling. Store in a cool, dark place.

gooseberry and elderflower jam

Pale green gooseberries and fragrant elderflowers make perfect partners in this sharp, aromatic, intensely flavoured jam. The jam turns an unexpected pink colour during cooking.

Makes about 2kg/4½lb

INGREDIENTS

1.3kg/3lb/12 cups firm gooseberries, topped and tailed

300ml/½ pint/1¼ cups water

1.3kg/3lb/6½ cups granulated sugar, warmed

juice of 1 lemon

2 handfuls of elderflowers removed from their stalks

COOK'S TIP

The time taken to reach setting point will vary depending on the ripeness of the gooseberries. The riper the fruit, the longer the jam will need to be cooked to reach setting point.

1 Put the gooseberries into a large preserving pan, add the water and bring the mixture to the boil.

2 Cover the pan with a lid and simmer gently for 20 minutes until the fruit is soft. Using a potato masher, gently mash the fruit to crush it lightly.

3 Add the sugar, lemon juice and elderflowers to the pan and stir over a low heat until the sugar has dissolved. Boil for 10 minutes, or to setting point (105°C/220°F). Remove from the heat, skim off any scum and cool for 5 minutes, then stir. Pot and seal, then leave to cool before labelling.

damson jam

Dark, plump damsons used to only be found growing in the wild, but today they are available commercially. They produce a deeply coloured and richly flavoured jam that makes a delicious treat spread on toasted English muffins or warm crumpets at tea time.

Makes about 2kg/4½lb

INGREDIENTS

1kg/2¼lb damsons or wild plums

1.4 litres/2¼ pints/6 cups water

1kg/2¼lb/5 cups preserving or granulated sugar, warmed

COOK'S TIP

It is important to seal the jars as soon as you have filled them to ensure the jam remains sterile. However, you should then leave the jars to cool completely before labelling and storing them to avoid the risk of burns.

1 Put the damsons in a preserving pan and pour in the water. Bring to the boil. Reduce the heat and simmer gently until the damsons are soft, then stir in the sugar.

2 Bring the mixture to the boil, skimming off stones as they rise. Boil to setting point (105°C/220°F). Leave to cool for 10 minutes, then pot. Seal, then label and store when cool.

greengage and almond jam

This is the perfect preserve to make when greengages are readily available in stores, or if you find you have a glut of the fruit. It has a gloriously rich, golden honey colour and a smooth texture that contrasts wonderfully with the little slivers of almond.

Makes about 1.3kg/3lb

INGREDIENTS

1.3kg/3lb greengages, stoned (pitted)

350ml/12fl oz/1½ cups water

juice of 1 lemon

50g/2oz/½ cup blanched almonds, cut into thin slivers

1.3kg/3lb/6½ cups granulated sugar, warmed

COOK'S TIP

Greengages look like unripened plums. However, despite their appearance, they have a wonderfully aromatic flavour that is captured perfectly in this delicious jam.

1 Put the greengages and water in a preserving pan with the lemon juice and almond slivers. Bring to the boil, then cover and simmer for 15–20 minutes, or until the greengages are really soft.

2 Add the sugar to the pan and stir over a low heat until the sugar has dissolved. Bring to the boil and cook for 10–15 minutes, or until the jam reaches setting point (105°C/220°F).

3 Remove the pan from the heat and skim off any scum from the surface using a slotted spoon.

4 Leave to cool for 10 minutes, then stir gently and pour into warmed sterilized jars. Seal, then leave to cool completely before labelling. Store in a cool place.

rhubarb and ginger jam

Late summer is the time to make this preserve, when rhubarb leaves are enormous and the stalks thick and green. It has a wonderfully tart, tangy flavour and is delicious spooned over plain cake, or used as a filling with whipped cream.

Makes about 2kg/4½lb

INGREDIENTS

1kg/2¼lb rhubarb

1kg/2¼lb/5 cups preserving
  or granulated sugar

25g/1oz fresh root ginger, bruised

115g/4oz crystallized ginger

50g/2oz/¼ cup candied orange
  peel, chopped

COOK'S TIP

The young, slender rhubarb stems that are available in the spring are more suitable for making tarts and pies. Their delicate flavour does not shine through in preserves, so it is worth waiting until later in the season for mature rhubarb.

1 Cut the rhubarb into short pieces and layer with the sugar in a glass bowl. Leave to stand overnight.

2 The next day, scrape the rhubarb and sugar mixture into a large, heavy preserving pan.

3 Tie the bruised ginger root in a piece of muslin (cheesecloth) and add it to the rhubarb. Cook gently for 30 minutes, or until the rhubarb has softened.

4 Remove the root ginger from the pan and stir in the crystallized ginger and candied orange peel.

5 Bring the mixture to the boil, then cook over a high heat until setting point is reached (105°C/220°F). Leave to cool for a few minutes, then pour into warmed sterilized jars and seal. When completely cool, label and store.

papaya and apricot jam

Apricots and papaya make perfect partners in this tantalizing jam. However, if you prefer plain apricot jam, simply replace the papaya with the same weight of apricots.

2 Slice the apricots and place in a preserving pan with the kernels, papaya, grated lemon rind and juice and the water. Bring to the boil then cover and simmer for 20–30 minutes, or until the fruit is really tender.

Makes about 1.3kg/3lb

INGREDIENTS

900g/2lb stoned (pitted) apricots,
  6 stones (pits) reserved

450g/1lb papaya, peeled, seeded and
  cut into small chunks

grated rind and juice of 2 lemons

250ml/8fl oz/1 cup water

1.3kg/3lb/6½ cups granulated
  sugar, warmed

COOK'S TIP

The bitter kernels from apricot stones contribute an almond-like flavour to the jam. Only a few should be used as they have a strong flavour. They are blanched to remove natural toxins.

1 Using a nut cracker or wooden mallet, crack the reserved apricot stones and remove the kernels inside. Put the kernels in a pan, pour over boiling water and cook for 2 minutes, then drain and slide off their skins.

3 Add the sugar to the pan and stir continuously over a low heat until the sugar has dissolved. Bring to the boil and cook for about 15 minutes, or until the jam reaches setting point (105°C/220°F).

4 Remove the pan from the heat and skim off any scum from the surface using a slotted spoon. Cool for 5 minutes, then stir gently and pour into warmed sterilized jars and seal. When cool, label the jars, then store in a cool, dark place.

melon and star anise jam

The delicate flavour of melon is brought out by spicy ginger and perfectly complemented by aromatic star anise. Once opened, store this delicious jam in the refrigerator.

Makes about 1.3kg/3lb

INGREDIENTS

2 Charentais or cantaloupe melons, peeled and seeded

450g/1lb/2¼ cups granulated sugar

2 star anise

4 pieces preserved stem ginger in syrup, drained and finely chopped

finely grated rind and juice of 2 lemons

1 Cut the melons into small cubes and layer with the granulated sugar in a large non-metallic bowl. Cover with clear film (plastic wrap) and leave overnight, or until the melons release their juices.

2 Pour the melon and sugar mixture into a large pan and add the star anise, chopped ginger, lemon rind and juice and stir to combine.

3 Bring the mixture to the boil, then lower the heat. Simmer for 25 minutes, or until the melon has become transparent and the setting point reached (105°C/220°F).

4 Spoon the jam into hot sterilized jars and seal. Leave to cool, then label and store in a cool, dark place.

COOK'S TIP

To test for the set, spoon a little jam on to a chilled plate. It should wrinkle when pushed with a finger.

sweet fruit jellies

Sparkling, jewel-like sweet fruit jellies make a wonderful alternative to jams and conserves, spread on toast or crumpets, or spooned over ice cream in place of a sauce. The fruit is cooked gently for as short a time as possible, then strained through muslin to obtain the clear liquid. Jellies give a lower yield than jam but they really capture the true flavour of fruits and are a lovely way to preserve.

hedgerow jelly

In the autumn, hedgerows are laden with damsons, blackberries and elderberries and it is well worth spending an afternoon in the countryside picking fruit to make into this delightful jelly.

Makes about 1.3kg/3lb

INGREDIENTS

450g/1lb damsons, washed
450g/1lb/4 cups blackberries, washed
225g/8oz/2 cups raspberries
225g/8oz/2 cups elderberries, washed
juice and pips (seeds) of 2 large lemons
about 1.3kg/3lb/6½ cups preserving
  or granulated sugar, warmed

COOK'S TIP

If you do not have enough of one fruit, you can vary the quantities as long as the total weight of fruit is the same.

2 Mash the fruit and leave to cool slightly. Pour into a scalded jelly bag suspended over a non-metallic bowl and leave to drain overnight.

3 Measure the strained juice into a preserving pan. Add 450g/1lb/ 2¼ cups sugar for every 600ml/ 1 pint/2½ cups strained fruit juice.

4 Heat the mixture, stirring, over a low heat until the sugar has dissolved. Increase the heat and boil rapidly without stirring for 10–15 minutes, or until the jelly reaches setting point (105°C/220°F).

1 Put the fruit, lemon juice and pips in a large pan. Pour over just enough water to cover. Put a lid on the pan and simmer for 1 hour.

5 Remove the pan from the heat and skim off any scum using a slotted spoon. Ladle into warmed, sterilized jars and seal. Leave to cool, then label and store.

mulberry jelly

Deep red mulberries are not often available but if you have access to a tree you will find they make the most wonderful jellies and jams. For a good set, pick the fruits when they are red.

Makes about 900g/2lb

INGREDIENTS

900g/2lb/8 cups unripe red mulberries
grated rind and juice of 1 lemon
600ml/1 pint/2½ cups water
about 900g/2lb/4½ cups preserving
  or granulated sugar, warmed

1 Put the mulberries in a pan with the lemon rind and juice and the water. Bring to the boil, cover and simmer for 1 hour, then remove from the heat and leave to cool.

2 Pour the fruit into a scalded jelly bag suspended over a non-metallic bowl and leave to drain overnight.

3 Measure the strained juice into a preserving pan. Add 450g/1lb/ 2¼ cups sugar for every 600ml/ 1 pint/2½ cups fruit juice.

4 Heat the mixture over a low heat, stirring, until the sugar has completely dissolved. Increase the heat and boil rapidly, without stirring, for 5–10 minutes, or to setting point (105°C/220°F).

5 Skim off any scum from the surface of the jelly using a slotted spoon. Ladle into warmed, sterilized jars, cover and seal. When the jars are completely cool, label, then store in a cool, dark place.

COOK'S TIPS

• To test for the set, spoon a little jelly on to a chilled saucer. Chill for about 3 minutes, then gently push the jelly with your finger; if the surface wrinkles, the jelly has reached setting point and it is ready to bottle.

• To make redcurrant jelly using the method here, measure the same quantity of fruit, but add slightly less sugar to the strained juice: 450g/ 1lb/1¼ cups sugar for every 600ml/ 1 pint/2½ cups juice.

cranberry jelly

This clear, well-flavoured preserve has a tart flavour and is absolutely delicious served with freshly baked scones, toasted tea cakes and crumpets, or as a glaze for fruit tarts. It can also be served at Christmas with a festive roast turkey, pheasant or guinea fowl.

Makes about 900g/2lb

INGREDIENTS

900g/2lb/8 cups cranberries

450g/1lb sweet eating apples, washed and chopped with skins and cores intact

grated rind and juice of 1 orange

600ml/1 pint/2½ cups water

about 900g/2lb/4½ cups preserving or granulated sugar, warmed

COOK'S TIP

Do not be tempted to squeeze the jelly bag while it is draining or the jelly will become cloudy.

1 Put the cranberries and apples in a pan with the orange rind, juice and water. Bring to the boil then cover and simmer for 1 hour.

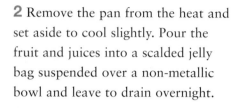

2 Remove the pan from the heat and set aside to cool slightly. Pour the fruit and juices into a scalded jelly bag suspended over a non-metallic bowl and leave to drain overnight.

3 Measure the strained juice into a preserving pan. Add 450g/1lb/2¼ cups sugar for every 600ml/1 pint/2½ cups strained juice.

4 Heat, stirring, over a low heat until the sugar has dissolved completely. Increase the heat and boil rapidly, without stirring, for 5–10 minutes, or until the jelly reaches setting point (105°C/220°F).

5 Remove the pan from the heat and skim off any scum from the surface using a slotted spoon. Ladle into warmed, sterilized jars, cover and seal. Leave to cool, then label and store in a cool, dark place.

red plum and cardamom jelly

The fragrance of warm, spicy cardamom combines wonderfully with all varieties of plum – red plums with a good tart flavour are perfect for making into this sweet, fruity, aromatic jelly. Serve it with plain rich ice creams and custards or spread it on toast for breakfast.

Makes about 1.8kg/4lb

INGREDIENTS

1.8kg/4lb red plums, stoned (pitted)

10ml/2 tsp crushed green
  cardamom pods

600ml/1 pint/2½ cups red grape juice

150ml/¼ pint/⅔ cup water

about 1.3kg/3lb/6½ cups preserving
  or granulated sugar, warmed

1 Put the plums, cardamom pods, grape juice and water in a large pan. Bring to the boil, then cover and simmer gently for 1 hour. Leave to cool slightly, then pour into a scalded jelly bag suspended over a non-metallic bowl and leave to drain overnight.

2 Measure the strained juice into a preserving pan. Add 450g/1lb/2¼ cups sugar for every 600ml/1 pint/2½ cups strained juice.

3 Heat the mixture over a low heat, stirring constantly until the sugar has dissolved completely. Increase the heat and boil, without stirring, for 10–15 minutes, or until the jelly reaches setting point (105°C/220°F).

4 Remove the pan from the heat and skim off any scum. Spoon the jelly into warmed sterilized jars, cover and seal. When cool, label and store in a cool, dark place.

rosehip and apple jelly

This economical jelly is made with windfall apples and wild rosehips. It is rich in vitamin C, full of flavour, and excellent spread on freshly toasted crumpets or scones.

Makes about 2kg/4½lb

INGREDIENTS

1kg/2¼lb windfall apples, peeled, trimmed and quartered

450g/1lb firm, ripe rosehips

about 1.3kg/3lb/6½ cups preserving or granulated sugar, warmed

1 Place the quartered apples in a large pan with just enough water to cover, plus 300ml/½ pint/ 1¼ cups of extra water.

COOK'S TIP

There is no need to remove all the peel from the apples: simply cut out any bruised, damaged or bad areas.

2 Bring the mixture to the boil and cook gently until the apples soften and turn to a pulp. Meanwhile, chop the rosehips coarsely. Add the rosehips to the pan with the apple and simmer for 10 minutes.

3 Remove from the heat and stand for 10 minutes, then pour the mixture into a scalded jelly bag suspended over a non-metallic bowl and leave to drain overnight.

4 Measure the juice into a preserving pan and bring to the boil. Add 400g/14oz/2 cups warmed sugar for each 600ml/ 1 pint/2½ cups of liquid. Stir until the sugar has completely dissolved. Boil to setting point (105°C/220°F).

5 Pour the jelly into warmed, sterilized jars and seal. Label and store when completely cold.

spiced cider and apple jelly

This wonderful spicy jelly has a rich, warming flavour, making it ideal to serve during the cold winter months. Serve as a spread or use it to sweeten apple pies and desserts.

Makes about 1.3kg/3lb

INGREDIENTS

900g/2lb cooking apples, coarsely chopped with skins and cores intact

900ml/1¼ pints/3¾ cups sweet (hard) cider

juice and pips (seeds) of 2 oranges

1 cinnamon stick

6 whole cloves

150ml/½ pint/⅔ cup water

about 900g/2lb/4½ cups preserving or granulated sugar, warmed

2 Leave to cool slightly, then pour the fruit into a scalded jelly bag suspended over a non-metallic bowl and leave to drain overnight.

3 Measure the strained juice into a preserving pan. Add 450g/1lb/2¼ cups warmed sugar for every 600ml/1 pint/2½ cups juice.

4 Heat, stirring, over a low heat until the sugar has dissolved. Increase the heat and boil, without stirring, for 10 minutes, or until the jelly reaches setting point (105°C/220°F).

5 Remove from the heat and skim off any scum. Ladle into warmed sterilized jars. Cover, seal and label.

1 Put the apples, cider, juice and pips, cinnamon, cloves and water in a large pan. Bring to the boil, cover and simmer for about 1 hour.

quince and coriander jelly

When raw, quinces are inedible but once cooked and sweetened they become aromatic and have a wonderful flavour, which is enhanced here by the addition of warm, spicy coriander seeds.

2 Leave the fruit to cool slightly, then pour into a scalded jelly bag suspended over a non-metallic bowl and leave to drain overnight.

3 Measure the strained juice into a preserving pan. Add 450g/1lb/ 2¼ cups warmed sugar for every 600ml/1 pint/2½ cups juice.

4 Heat, stirring, over a low heat until the sugar has completely dissolved. Increase the heat and boil rapidly, without stirring, for 5–10 minutes or until the jelly reaches setting point (105°C/220°F).

5 Remove the pan from the heat and skim off any scum from the surface using a slotted spoon. Ladle into warmed sterilized jars, cover and seal. When cold, label and store in a cool, dark place.

COOK'S TIP

Jellies can look very pretty served in decorative glasses. Bottle the jelly in jars as above, then, when ready to serve, gently heat the jelly in a pan with a very small amount of water until melted. Pour the jelly into a heatproof glass and leave to set before serving.

Makes about 900g/2lb

INGREDIENTS

1kg/2¼lb quinces, washed and coarsely
chopped with skins and cores intact
15ml/1 tbsp coriander seeds
juice and pips (seeds) of 2 large lemons
900ml/1½ pints/3¾ cups water
about 900g/2lb/4½ cups preserving
or granulated sugar, warmed

VARIATION

If you don't have enough quinces, you can make up the quantity with apples. The flavour won't be quite the same but the jelly will still be delicious.

1 Put the quinces in a pan with the coriander seeds, lemon juice and pips, and the water. Bring to the boil, cover and simmer gently for about 1½ hours.

scented geranium and pear jelly

This jelly uses the leaves of scented geranium to give an aromatic lift to the pears. Use rose-scented leaves if you have them, otherwise add a couple of drops of rose water to the strained juice.

Makes about 900g/2lb

INGREDIENTS

900g/2lb Comice pears, washed and coarsely chopped with skins and cores intact

7 rose-scented geranium leaves, plus extra for storing

juice and pips (seeds) of 1 lemon

60ml/4 tbsp clear honey

900ml/1½ pints/3¾ cups water

about 900g/2lb/4½ cups preserving or granulated sugar, warmed

2 Remove the pan from the heat and leave to cool slightly. Pour the fruit into a scalded jelly bag suspended over a non-metallic bowl and leave to drain overnight.

3 Measure the strained juice into a preserving pan. Add 450g/1lb/ 2¼ cups warmed sugar for every 600ml/1 pint/2½ cups juice.

4 Heat, stirring, over a low heat until the sugar has dissolved. Increase the heat and boil rapidly, without stirring, for 10 minutes, or to setting point (105°C/220°F).

5 Remove the pan from the heat and skim off any scum using a slotted spoon. Place a blanched geranium leaf into each warmed sterilized jar, then ladle in the jelly. Cover and seal, then label.

1 Put the pears, geranium leaves, lemon juice, honey and water in a large pan. Bring to the boil, then cover and simmer for 1 hour.

clementine and lemon balm jelly

This sweet, aromatic jelly makes a delicious alternative to marmalade at breakfast. Clementines are the smallest of the tangerine family and have the most zesty skin and aromatic flesh.

Makes about 900g/2lb

INGREDIENTS

900g/2lb clementines, washed and coarsely chopped

450g/1lb tart cooking apples, coarsely chopped, with skins and cores intact

2 large sprigs of lemon balm or 1 lemon grass stalk, crushed

900ml/1½ pints/3¾ cups water

about 900g/2lb/4½ cups preserving or granulated sugar, warmed

COOK'S TIP

To prepare the lemon grass, you only need to crush the bulbous end of the stalk. Using the end of a rolling pin, gently bash the bulbous end of the stalk, then add to the pan. This helps to release its fragrant, zesty flavour into the jelly.

1 Put the fruit, lemon balm or lemon grass and water in a pan. Bring to the boil, cover and simmer for 1 hour until the fruit is soft. Cool slightly, then pour into a scalded jelly bag over a bowl and leave to drain overnight.

2 Measure the juice into a pan. Add 450g/1lb/2¼ cups sugar for every 600ml/1 pint/2½ cups juice.

3 Heat gently, stirring until the sugar has dissolved. Increase the heat and boil, without stirring, for 5–10 minutes, or until the jelly reaches setting point (105°C/220°F).

4 Remove the pan from the heat and skim off any scum using a slotted spoon. Pour into warmed sterilized jars, cover and seal. Label and store in a cool place.

muscat grape jelly

The wonderful perfumed flavour of Muscat grapes produces a deliciously fragrant, scented jelly. Do not be tempted to use other grapes because they will not give the same result.

Makes about 900g/2lb

INGREDIENTS

900g/2lb/6 cups Muscat grapes, washed and halved

juice and pips (seeds) of 2 lemons

600ml/1 pint/2½ cups water

30ml/2 tbsp elderflower cordial

about 900g/2lb/4½ cups preserving or granulated sugar, warmed

1 Place the grapes in a pan with the lemon juice and pips, and water. Bring to the boil, cover and simmer for 1½ hours. Cool slightly.

2 Mash the grapes, then pour the mixture into a scalded jelly bag suspended over a non-metallic bowl and leave to drain overnight.

3 Measure the juice into a pan and pour in the elderflower cordial. Add 450g/1lb/2¼ cups sugar for every 600ml/1 pint/2½ cups juice. Heat gently, stirring, until the sugar has dissolved. Increase the heat and boil, without stirring, for 5–10 minutes, or until the jelly reaches setting point (105°C/220°F).

4 Remove the pan from the heat and skim off any scum. Ladle into warmed sterilized jars. Cover, seal and label. Store in a cool place.

pineapple and passion fruit jelly

This exotic jelly has a wonderful warming glow to its taste and appearance. For the best-flavoured jelly, use a tart-tasting, not too ripe pineapple rather than a very ripe, sweet one.

Makes about 900g/2lb

INGREDIENTS

1 large pineapple, peeled, topped and tailed and coarsely chopped

4 passion fruit, halved, with seeds and pulp scooped out

900ml/1½ pints/3¾ cups water

about 900g/2lb/4½ cups preserving or granulated sugar, warmed

COOK'S TIP

For the best flavour, choose passion fruits with dark, wrinkled skins.

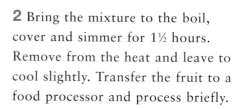

1 Place the pineapple and the passion fruit seeds and pulp in a large pan with the water.

2 Bring the mixture to the boil, cover and simmer for 1½ hours. Remove from the heat and leave to cool slightly. Transfer the fruit to a food processor and process briefly.

3 Pour the fruit pulp and any juices from the pan, into a scalded jelly bag suspended over a non-metallic bowl and leave to drain overnight.

4 Measure the strained juice into a preserving pan and add 450g/1lb/2¼ cups warmed sugar for every 600ml/1 pint/2½ cups juice.

5 Heat gently, stirring, until the sugar has dissolved. Increase the heat and boil rapidly, without stirring, for 10–15 minutes or to setting point (105°C/220°F).

6 Remove the pan from the heat and skim off any scum using a slotted spoon. Ladle the jelly into warmed sterilized jars, cover and seal. When cool, label and store in a cool, dark place.

pomegranate and grenadine jelly

The slightly tart flavoured, jewel-like flesh of the pomegranate makes the most wonderful jelly. Be careful though, because pomegranate juice can stain indelibly when spilt on clothing.

Makes about 900g/2lb

INGREDIENTS

6 ripe red pomegranates, peeled and seeds removed from membranes

120ml/4fl oz/½ cup grenadine syrup

juice and pips (seeds) of 2 oranges

300ml/½ pint/1¼ cups water

about 900g/2lb/4½ cups preserving or granulated sugar, warmed

1 Put the pomegranate seeds in bowl and crush to release their juice. Transfer them to a pan and add the grenadine, orange juice, pips and water.

2 Bring the mixture to the boil, cover and simmer for 1½ hours. Mash the fruit and leave to cool slightly, then pour into a scalded jelly bag suspended over a bowl and leave to drain overnight.

3 Measure the juice into a pan and add 450g/1lb/2¼ cups sugar for every 600ml/1 pint/2½ cups juice.

4 Heat, stirring, over a low heat until the sugar has dissolved. Increase the heat and boil rapidly, without stirring, for 5–10 minutes, or until the jelly reaches setting point (105°C/220°F).

5 Remove the pan from the heat and skim off any scum. Ladle into warmed sterilized jars, cover, seal and label. Store in a cool place.

marmalades

These classic preserves come somewhere between a jam and a jelly and are traditionally served for breakfast. Usually made of citrus fruits, marmalades have a jelly base with small pieces of fruit suspended in it. They can be tart and bitter with thick cut shreds of peel, or sweet with thinly cut zest. The Seville orange is favoured because of its refreshing tang and high pectin content but any citrus fruit can be used, as long as its shredded rind is cooked until very tender. All the recipes in this chapter will keep for at least 1 year.

oxford marmalade

The characteristic caramel colour and rich flavour of a traditional Oxford marmalade is obtained by cutting the fruit coarsely and cooking it for several hours before adding the sugar.

Makes about 2.25kg/5lb

INGREDIENTS

900g/2lb Seville (Temple) oranges
1.75 litres/3 pints/7½ cups water
1.3kg/3lb/6½ cups granulated sugar, warmed

COOK'S TIP

Traditionalists say that only bitter oranges such as Seville should be used to make marmalade. Although this isn't always true, it is most certainly the case when making Oxford marmalade.

1 Scrub the orange skins, then remove the rind using a vegetable peeler. Thickly slice the rind and put in a large pan.

2 Chop the fruit, reserving the pips (seeds), and add to the rind in the pan, along with the water. Tie the orange pips in a piece of muslin (cheesecloth) and add to the pan. Bring to the boil, then cover and simmer for 2 hours. Add more water during cooking to maintain the same volume. Remove the pan from the heat and leave overnight.

3 The next day, remove the muslin bag from the oranges, squeezing well, and return the pan to the heat. Bring to the boil, then cover and simmer for 1 hour.

4 Add the warmed sugar to the pan, then slowly bring the mixture to the boil, stirring until the sugar has dissolved completely. Increase the heat and boil rapidly for about 15 minutes, or until setting point is reached (105°C/220°F).

5 Remove the pan from the heat and skim off any scum from the surface. Leave to cool for about 5 minutes, stir, then pour into warmed sterilized jars and seal. When cold, label, then store in a cool, dark place.

st clement's marmalade

*This classic preserve made from oranges and lemons has a lovely citrus tang. It has a light,
refreshing flavour and is perfect for serving for breakfast, spread on freshly toasted bread.*

Makes about 2.25kg/5lb

INGREDIENTS

450g/1lb Seville (Temple) oranges

450g/1lb sweet oranges

4 lemons

1.5 litres/2½ pints/6¼ cups water

1.2kg/2½lb/5½ cups granulated sugar,
  warmed

1 Wash the oranges and lemons,
then halve and squeeze the juice
into a large pan. Tie the pips
(seeds) and membranes in a muslin
(cheesecloth) bag, shred the orange
and lemon rind and add to the pan.

2 Add the water to the pan, bring
to the boil, then cover and simmer
for 2 hours. Remove the muslin
bag, leave to cool, then squeeze
any liquid back into the pan.

3 Add the warmed sugar to the
pan and stir over a low heat until
completely dissolved. Bring to the
boil and boil rapidly for about
15 minutes or until the marmalade
reaches setting point (105°C/220°F).

4 Remove the pan from the heat
and skim off any scum from the
surface. Leave to cool for about
5 minutes, stir, then pour into
warmed sterilized jars and seal.
When cold, label, then store in a
cool, dark place.

pink grapefruit and cranberry marmalade

Cranberries give this glorious marmalade an extra tartness and a full fruit flavour, as well as an inimitable vibrant colour. The resulting preserve makes a lively choice for breakfast or a brilliant accompaniment for cold roast turkey during the festive season.

Makes about 2.25kg/5lb

INGREDIENTS

675g/1½lb pink grapefruit
juice and pips (seeds) of 2 lemons
900ml/1½ pints/3¾ cups water
225g/8oz/2 cups cranberries
1.3kg/3lb/6½ cups granulated sugar, warmed

COOK'S TIP

You can use fresh or frozen cranberries to make this marmalade. Either gives equally good results.

1 Wash, halve and quarter the grapefruit, then slice them thinly, reserving the pips (seeds) and any juice that runs out.

2 Tie the grapefruit and lemon pips in a muslin (cheesecloth) bag and place in a large pan with the grapefruit slices and lemon juice.

3 Add the water and bring to the boil. Cover and simmer gently for 1½–2 hours, or until the grapefruit rind is very tender. Remove the muslin bag, leave to cool, then squeeze over the pan.

4 Add the cranberries to the pan, then bring to the boil. Simmer for 15–20 minutes, or until the berries have popped and softened.

5 Add the sugar to the pan and stir over a low heat until the sugar has completely dissolved. Bring to the boil and boil rapidly for about 10 minutes, or until setting point is reached (105°C/220°F).

6 Remove the pan from the heat and skim off any scum from the surface using a slotted spoon. Leave to cool for 5–10 minutes, then stir and pour into warmed sterilized jars. Seal, then label when the marmalade is cold.

ruby red grapefruit marmalade

If you prefer a really tangy marmalade, grapefruit is the perfect choice. To achieve a wonderfully red-blushed preserve, look for the red variety rather than pink. They have a wonderful flavour and make a really delicious, sweet, jewel-coloured preserve.

Makes about 1.8kg/4lb

INGREDIENTS

900g/2lb ruby red grapefruit

1 lemon

1.2 litres/2 pints/5 cups water

1.3kg/3lb/6½ cups granulated sugar, warmed

1 Wash the grapefruit and lemon and remove the rind in thick pieces using a vegetable peeler. Cut the fruit in half and squeeze the juice into a preserving pan, reserving all the pips (seeds).

2 Put the pips and membranes from the fruit in a muslin (cheesecloth) bag and add to the pan. Discard the grapefruit and lemon shells.

3 Using a sharp knife, cut the grapefruit and lemon rind into thin or coarse shreds, as preferred, and place in the pan.

COOK'S TIP

Although you can use yellow grapefruit to make this marmalade, it tends to give a very pale result with more tang than the ruby red variety, but a much less fruity flavour.

4 Add the water to the pan and bring to the boil. Cover and simmer for 2 hours, or until the rind is very tender.

5 Remove the muslin bag from the pan, leave to cool, then squeeze it over the pan. Add the sugar and stir over a low heat until it has dissolved. Bring to the boil, then boil rapidly for 10–15 minutes, or to setting point (105°C/220°F).

6 Remove the pan from the heat and skim off any scum using a slotted spoon. Leave to cool for about 10 minutes, then stir and pour into warmed sterilized jars. Seal, then label when cold.

lemon and ginger marmalade

This combination of lemon and ginger produces a really zesty and versatile preserve, perfect served on toast at any time of day. It is also excellent added to meat glazes. Mix a few spoonfuls of the marmalade with a little soy sauce and brush over meat before grilling.

Makes about 1.8kg/4lb

INGREDIENTS

1.2kg/2½lb lemons

150g/5oz fresh root ginger, peeled and finely grated

1.2 litres/2 pints/5 cups water

900g/2lb/4½ cups granulated sugar, warmed

COOK'S TIP

When choosing fresh root ginger, select young, firm, fine-skinned pieces. For the best results, grate only the tender, juicy parts of the root and discard any tough, hairy parts.

1 Quarter and slice the lemons. Tie the pips (seeds) in a muslin (cheesecloth) bag and place in a preserving pan with the lemons, ginger and water. Bring to the boil, cover with a lid and simmer for 2 hours, or until the fruit is tender.

2 Remove the muslin bag from the pan, leave to cool then squeeze over the pan to release all the juice and pectin. Stir in the sugar over a low heat until dissolved, then increase the heat and boil for 5–10 minutes, or until setting point is reached (105°C/220°F).

3 Remove the pan from the heat and skim off any scum from the surface using a slotted spoon.

4 Leave to cool for 5 minutes, stir, then pour into warmed sterilized jars and seal. When cold, label and store in a cool place.

orange and coriander marmalade

This traditional marmalade made with bitter Seville oranges has the added zing of warm, spicy coriander. Cut the orange rind into thin or coarse shreds, according to taste.

Makes about 1.8kg/4lb

INGREDIENTS

675g/1½lb Seville (Temple) oranges

2 lemons

15ml/1 tbsp crushed coriander seeds

1.5 litres/2½ pints/6¼ cups water

900g/2lb/4½ cups granulated sugar, warmed

1 Cut the oranges and lemons in half and squeeze out all the juice. Place the orange and lemon pips (seeds) in a muslin (cheesecloth) bag. Using a sharp knife, cut the rind into shreds and place in a preserving pan with the juice.

2 Put the coriander seeds in the muslin bag with the pips and place in the pan. Add the water and bring to the boil. Cover and simmer for 2 hours, or until the mixture has reduced by half and the peel is soft.

3 Remove the muslin bag from the pan. Set it aside to cool, then squeeze it over the pan to release all the juices and pectin.

4 Add the sugar to the pan and stir over a low heat until it has dissolved. Bring to the boil and boil rapidly for 5–10 minutes, or to setting point (105°C/220°F).

5 Remove the pan from the heat and skim off any scum from the surface using a slotted spoon. Leave to cool for 5 minutes, stir then pour into warmed sterilized jars. Seal, then label when cold.

orange and whisky marmalade

Adding whisky to orange marmalade gives it a fantastic warmth and flavour. The whisky is stirred in after the marmalade is cooked, to retain its strength and slightly bitter edge, which would be lost if boiled. Whisky marmalade is great spooned over a steamed sponge pudding.

3 Remove the muslin bag from the pan, leave to cool, then squeeze it over the pan to release any juice and pectin. Add the sugar, then stir over a low heat until the sugar has dissolved. Increase the heat and boil for 5–10 minutes until setting point is reached (105°C/220°F).

4 Remove the pan from the heat and skim off any scum from the surface using a slotted spoon. Stir in the whisky, then leave to cool for 5 minutes. Stir and pour the marmalade into warmed sterilized jars. Seal, then label when cold. Store in a cool dark place.

Makes about 2.25kg/5lb

INGREDIENTS

900g/2lb Seville (Temple) oranges

juice and pips (seeds) of 1 large lemon

1.2 litres/2 pints/5 cups water

1.5kg/3lb 6oz/7½ cups granulated sugar, warmed

60ml/4 tbsp whisky

1 Scrub the oranges and cut in half. Squeeze the juice into a large pan, reserving the pips (seeds) and any membranes. Place these in a muslin (cheesecloth) bag with the lemon pips and add to the juice.

2 Using a sharp knife, thinly slice the orange rind and put in the pan along with the water. Bring to the boil, then cover and simmer for 1½–2 hours, or until the citrus rind is very tender.

fine lime shred marmalade

There is something about lime marmalade that really captures the flavour and essence of the fruit. It is important to cut the slices very finely though, because lime skins tend to be tougher than those on any other citrus fruit and can result in a chewy marmalade if cut thickly.

Makes about 2.25kg/5lb

INGREDIENTS

12 limes
4 kaffir lime leaves
1.2 litres/2 pints/5 cups water
1.3kg/3lb/6½ cups granulated sugar, warmed

1 Halve the limes lengthways, then slice thinly, reserving any pips (seeds). Tie the pips and lime leaves in a muslin (cheesecloth) bag and place the bag in a large pan with the sliced fruit.

2 Add the water to the pan and bring to the boil. Cover and simmer gently for 1½–2 hours, or until the rind is very soft. Remove the muslin bag, leave to cool, then squeeze it over the pan to release any juice and pectin.

COOK'S TIP

To check whether the rind is cooked, remove a piece from the pan (before the sugar is added) and leave it to cool briefly. When cool enough to handle, press the rind between finger and thumb – it should be very soft.

3 Add the sugar to the pan, and stir over a low heat until the sugar has dissolved. Bring to the boil, then boil rapidly for 15 minutes, stirring occasionally, until setting point is reached (105°C/220°F).

4 Remove the pan from the heat and skim off any scum. Leave to cool for 5 minutes, stir, then pour into warmed sterilized jars. Seal, then label when cold. Store in a cool, dark place.

COOK'S TIPS

• To check for setting, spoon a little marmalade on to a chilled saucer and chill for 2 minutes. Push the surface with your finger; if wrinkles form, the marmalade is ready to bottle.
• Stirring marmalade after standing and before potting distributes the fruit rind evenly as the preserve begins to set.

tangerine and lemon grass marmalade

The subtle flavours of lemon grass and kaffir lime leaves add an exotic edge to this marmalade.
You can also stir in thinly shredded lime leaf before bottling, which gives a very pretty result.

2 Tie all the pips, lemon grass and lime leaves in a piece of muslin (cheesecloth) and add to the pan. Boil, then simmer for 1½–2 hours, or until the tangerine rind is soft. Remove the bag, leave to cool, then squeeze over the pan.

3 Stir in the sugar over a low heat until completely dissolved, then boil for 5–10 minutes, or to setting point (105°C/220°F).

4 Remove the pan from the heat and skim off any scum. Leave to cool for 5 minutes, then stir and pour into warmed sterilized jars. Seal, then label when cold.

Makes about 1.8kg/4lb

INGREDIENTS

900g/2lb tangerines, washed and halved

juice and pips (seeds) of 2 Seville (Temple) oranges

900ml/1½ pints/3¾ cups water

2 lemon grass sticks, halved and crushed

3 kaffir lime leaves

900g/2lb/4½ cups granulated sugar, warmed

COOK'S TIP

If you can't find kaffir lime leaves, you can substitute the finely pared rind of one lime.

1 Using a sharp knife, slice the tangerines thinly, reserving the pips. Place the sliced fruit in a preserving pan, along with juice from the Seville oranges and the measured water.

pomelo and pineapple marmalade

Slightly larger than a grapefruit, pomelos have lime-green skin and a sharp, refreshing flavour and are delicious combined with tangy pineapple. Serve as a spread or spoon over desserts.

Makes about 2.75kg/6lb

INGREDIENTS

2 pomelos

900ml/1½ pints/3¾ cups water

2 x 432g/14¼oz cans crushed pineapple in fruit juice

900g/2lb/4½ cups granulated sugar, warmed

2 Cover the pan and simmer for 1½–2 hours, stirring occasionally, or until the fruit is soft. Add the pineapple and juice and simmer for a further 30 minutes.

3 Remove the muslin bag from the pan, leave to cool, then squeeze over the pan. Add the sugar and stir over a low heat until it has dissolved. Increase the heat and boil for 10 minutes, or to setting point (105°C/220°F).

4 Remove the pan from the heat and skim off any scum from the surface using a slotted spoon. Leave to cool for 10 minutes, then stir and pour into warmed sterilized jars. Seal, then label the jars when they are cold.

1 Wash and halve the pomelos. Squeeze out the juice, reserving any pips (seeds), and pour into a large pan. Remove the membranes and any excess pith and tie in muslin (cheesecloth) with the pips. Slice the peel thinly and add to the pan along with the muslin bag and water. Bring to the boil.

peach and kumquat marmalade

Combined with sweet, scented peaches, kumquats make a wonderful, fresh-tasting preserve.
This lovely marmalade has a jam-like consistency and is great at any time of day.

Makes about 1.8kg/4lb

INGREDIENTS

675g/1½lb kumquats, sliced thinly, pips (seeds) and juice reserved

juice and pips of 1 lime

900g/2lb peaches, skinned and thinly sliced, skins reserved

900ml/1½ pints/3¾ cups water

900g/2lb/4½ cups granulated sugar, warmed

1 Tie the pips and the peach skins in a muslin (cheesecloth) bag and put in a pan with the kumquats, juices and water. Bring to the boil, then cover and simmer for 50 minutes.

2 Add the peaches to the pan, bring to the boil, then simmer for 40–50 minutes, or until the fruit has become very soft. Remove the muslin bag, leave to cool, then squeeze over the pan.

3 Add the sugar to the pan and stir over a low heat until it has dissolved. Bring the mixture to the boil, then boil rapidly for about 15 minutes, stirring occasionally, to setting point (105°C/220°F).

4 Remove the pan from the heat and skim off any scum from the surface using a slotted spoon.

5 Leave to cool for 5–10 minutes, then stir and pour into warmed sterilized jars. Seal, then label when the jars are cold. Store in a cool, dark place.

apricot and orange marmalade

Serve this sweet marmalade with warm croissants and strong coffee for a leisurely weekend breakfast. The combination of oranges and rich-tasting apricots is a winner.

Makes about 1.5kg/3lb 6oz

INGREDIENTS

2 Seville (Temple) oranges, washed and quartered

1 lemon, washed and quartered

1.2 litres/2 pints/5 cups water

900g/2lb apricots, stoned (pitted) and thinly sliced

900g/2lb/4½ cups granulated sugar, warmed

COOK'S TIP

It is important to use a food processor to chop the oranges and lemon for this recipe. Chopping them this finely gives the marmalade its wonderful consistency. Preparing the fruits by hand will not give the same result.

1 Remove the pips (seeds) from the citrus fruit and tie in a muslin (cheesecloth) bag. Finely chop the oranges and lemons in a food processor and put in a large pan with the muslin bag and water.

2 Bring the mixture to the boil, then simmer, covered, for 1 hour.

3 Add the apricots to the pan, bring to the boil, then simmer for 30–40 minutes, or until the fruits are very tender.

4 Add the sugar to the pan and stir over a low heat until the sugar has dissolved. Bring to the boil, then boil rapidly for 15 minutes, stirring occasionally, until setting point is reached (105°C/220°F).

5 Remove the pan from the heat and skim off any scum from the surface using a slotted spoon. Leave to cool for about 5 minutes, then stir and pour into warmed sterilized jars. Seal, then label when cold. Store in a cool place.

curds, butters and cheeses

These smooth, thick, luscious preserves capture the colours and flavours of the season. Butters and curds are thick and spreadable, delicious spooned on to toast or griddle cakes. In contrast, cheeses are firmer and can be cut into wedges or slices, or set in small individual moulds. Serve them as a delicious accompaniment to roast meats or dairy cheeses, or cut into wedges, dredge in sugar and serve as a sweetmeat after the meal.

lemon curd

This classic tangy, creamy curd is still one of the most popular of all the curds. It is delicious spread thickly over freshly baked white bread or served with American-style pancakes, and also makes a wonderfully rich, zesty sauce spooned over fresh fruit tarts.

Makes about 450g/1lb

INGREDIENTS

3 lemons

200g/7oz/1 cup caster (superfine) sugar

115g/4oz/8 tbsp unsalted (sweet) butter, diced

2 large (US extra large) eggs

2 large (US extra large) egg yolks

1 Wash the lemons, then finely grate the rind and place in a large heatproof bowl. Using a sharp knife, halve the lemons and squeeze the juice into the bowl. Set over a pan of gently simmering water and add the sugar and butter. Stir until the sugar has dissolved and the butter melted.

2 Put the eggs and yolks in a bowl and beat together with a fork. Pour the eggs through a sieve into the lemon mixture, and whisk well until thoroughly combined.

3 Stir the mixture constantly over the heat until the lemon curd thickens and lightly coats the back of a wooden spoon.

4 Remove the pan from the heat and pour the curd into small, warmed sterilized jars. Cover, seal and label. Store in a cool, dark place, ideally in the refrigerator. Use within 3 months. (Once opened, store in the refrigerator.)

COOK'S TIP

If you are really impatient when it comes to cooking, it is possible to cook the curd in a heavy pan directly over a low heat. However, you really need to watch it like a hawk to avoid the mixture curdling. If the curd looks as though it's beginning to curdle, plunge the base of the pan in cold water and beat vigorously.

seville orange curd

Using flavoursome Seville oranges gives this curd a fantastic orange flavour and a real citrus tang. It is perfect for spreading on toast for breakfast or at tea time, and is also superlative folded into whipped cream and used as a filling for cakes, roulades and scones.

Makes about 450g/1lb

INGREDIENTS

2 Seville (Temple) oranges

115g/4oz/8 tbsp unsalted (sweet)
  butter, diced

200g/7oz/1 cup caster (superfine) sugar

2 large (US extra large) eggs

2 large (US extra large) egg yolks

1 Wash the oranges, then finely grate the rind and place in a large heatproof bowl. Halve the oranges and squeeze the juice into the bowl with the rind.

2 Place the bowl over a pan of gently simmering water and add the butter and sugar. Stir until the sugar has completely dissolved and the butter melted.

3 Put the eggs and yolks in a small bowl and lightly whisk, then pour into the orange mixture through a sieve. Whisk them together until thoroughly combined.

4 Stir the orange and egg mixture constantly over the heat until the mixture thickens and lightly coats the back of a wooden spoon.

5 Pour the orange curd into small, warmed sterilized jars, cover and seal. Store in a cool, dark place, preferably in the refrigerator.

WATCHPOINTS

• The very young, the elderly, pregnant women, and those with a compromised immune system are advised against eating raw eggs or food containing raw eggs. Although the eggs in fruit curds are lightly cooked, they may still be unsuitable for these groups of people.

• Fruit curds do not have the shelf-life of many other preserves and should be used within 3 months of making.

• Once opened, always store fruit curds in the refrigerator.

grapefruit curd

If you favour tangy and refreshing preserves, this grapefruit curd is the one to try. Really fresh free-range eggs give the best results and flavour when making curd.

Makes about 675g/1½lb

INGREDIENTS

finely grated rind and juice of 1 grapefruit

115g/4oz/8 tbsp unsalted (sweet) butter, diced

200g/7oz/1 cup caster (superfine) sugar

4 large (US extra large) eggs, lightly beaten

1 Put the grapefruit rind and juice in a large heatproof bowl with the butter and sugar, and set over a pan of gently simmering water. Heat the mixture, stirring occasionally, until the sugar has dissolved and the butter melted.

2 Add the beaten eggs to the fruit mixture, straining them through a sieve. Whisk together, then stir constantly over the heat until the mixture thickens and lightly coats the back of a wooden spoon.

3 Pour the curd into small, warmed sterilized jars, cover and seal. Label when the jars are cold. Store in a cool, dark place, preferably in the refrigerator and use within 3 months. (Once opened, store the curd in the refrigerator.)

VARIATION

Tangy grapefruit and sweet orange marry particularly well in creamy fruit curds. Add the grated rind of a small orange to this grapefruit recipe for an extra zingy, zesty alternative.

passion fruit curd

The tropical flavour and aroma of passion fruit fills this curd with a gloriously sunny character. It is perfect spread on toasted English muffins or little American pancakes.

Makes about 675g/1½lb

INGREDIENTS

grated rind and juice of 2 lemons

115g/4oz/8 tbsp unsalted (sweet) butter, diced

275g/10oz/1⅓ cups caster (superfine) sugar

4 passion fruit

4 eggs

2 egg yolks

1 Place the lemon rind and juice in a large heatproof bowl and add the butter and sugar.

2 Halve the passion fruit and scoop the seeds into a sieve set over the bowl. Press out all the juice and discard the seeds.

3 Place the bowl over a pan of gently simmering water and stir occasionally until the sugar has dissolved and the butter melted.

4 Beat the eggs and yolks together and add to the bowl, pouring them through a sieve, then whisk well to combine. Stir constantly until the mixture thickens and lightly coats the back of a spoon.

5 Pour the curd into small, warmed sterilized jars, cover and seal. Store in a cool, dark place, preferably in the refrigerator and use within 3 months. (Once opened, store in the refrigerator.)

apple and cinnamon butter

Fans of apple pies and crumbles will love this luscious apple butter. Serve on toast or with warmed brioche for a breakfast treat or with pancakes and cream for tea.

Makes about 1.8kg/4lb

INGREDIENTS

475ml/16fl oz/2 cups dry (hard) cider

450g/1lb tart cooking apples, peeled, cored and sliced

450g/1lb eating apples, peeled, cored and sliced

grated rind and juice of 1 lemon

675g/1½lb/scant 3½ cups granulated sugar, warmed

5ml/1 tsp ground cinnamon

COOK'S TIP

Leaving the butter to stand for 2 days give the flavours a chance to develop.

1 Pour the cider into a large pan and bring to the boil. Boil hard until the volume is reduced by half, then add the apples and lemon rind and juice.

2 Cover the pan and cook for 10 minutes. Uncover and continue cooking for 20–30 minutes, or until the apples are very soft.

3 Leave the mixture to cool slightly, then pour into a food processor or blender and blend to a purée. Press through a fine sieve into a bowl.

4 Measure the purée into a large heavy pan, adding 275g/10oz/ 1⅓ cups warmed sugar for every 600ml/1 pint/2½ cups of purée. Add the ground cinnamon and stir well to combine.

5 Gently heat the mixture, stirring continuously, until the sugar has completely dissolved. Increase the heat and boil steadily for about 20 minutes, stirring frequently, until the mixture forms a thick purée that hold its shape when spooned on to a cold plate.

6 Spoon the apple and cinnamon butter into warmed sterilized jars. Seal and label, then store in a cool, dark place for 2 days to allow the flavours to develop before serving.

pear and vanilla butter

The delicate flavour of pears is enhanced by vanilla in this butter that really captures the essence of the fruit. It is well worth allowing it to mature for a few days before eating.

Makes about 675g/1½lb

INGREDIENTS

900g/2lb pears, peeled, cored
  and chopped

juice of 3 lemons

300ml/½ pint/1¼ cups water

1 vanilla pod (bean), split

675g/1½lb/scant 3½ cups granulated
  sugar, warmed

1 Place the pears in a large pan with the lemon juice, water and vanilla pod. Bring to the boil, then cover and simmer for 10 minutes. Uncover the pan and continue cooking for a further 15–20 minutes, or until the pears are very soft.

2 Remove the vanilla pod from the pan, then carefully scrape the seeds into the fruit mixture using the tip of a knife.

3 Tip the fruit and juices into a food processor or blender and blend to a purée. Press the purée through a fine sieve into a bowl.

4 Measure the purée into a large heavy pan, adding 275g/10oz/ 1⅓ cups warmed sugar for every 600ml/1 pint/2½ cups of purée.

5 Stir the mixture over a low heat until the sugar dissolves. Increase the heat and boil for 15 minutes, stirring, until the mixture forms a thick purée that holds its shape when spooned on to a cold plate.

6 Spoon the pear butter into small, warmed sterilized jars. Seal, label and store in a cool, dark place for at least 2 days before serving.

COOK'S TIPS

• Fruit butters have a soft spreading consistency – thicker than fruit curds, but softer than fruit cheeses. They make an excellent tea time preserve.

• Fruit butters keep well in sealed jars and can be stored for up to 3 months. Once opened, they should be stored in the refrigerator.

pumpkin and maple butter

This all-American butter has a lovely bright, autumnal colour and flavour. It is perfect served spread on little pancakes fresh from the griddle, or used as a filling or topping for cakes.

Makes about 675g/1½lb

INGREDIENTS

1.2kg/2½lb pumpkin or butternut squash, peeled, seeded and chopped

450ml/¾ pint/scant 2 cups water

grated rind and juice of 1 orange

5ml/1 tsp ground cinnamon

120ml/4fl oz/½ cup maple syrup

675g/1½lb/scant 3½ cups granulated sugar, warmed

VARIATION

This butter is also delicious made with clear honey instead of maple syrup. It adds a distinctive flavour.

1 Put the pumpkin or squash in the pan with the water and cook for 30–40 minutes, or until it is very tender. Drain and, using the back of a spoon, press the cooked pumpkin or squash through a fine sieve into a bowl.

2 Stir the orange rind and juice, cinnamon and maple syrup into the purée, then measure the purée into a large pan, adding 275g/10oz/1⅓ cups warmed sugar for every 600ml/1 pint/2½ cups purée.

3 Gently heat the purée, stirring, until the sugar has dissolved. Increase the heat and boil for 10–20 minutes, stirring frequently, until the mixture forms a thick purée that holds its shape when spooned on to a cold plate.

4 Spoon the butter into small, warmed sterilized jars. Seal and label, then store in a cool, dark place for 2 days before eating.

mango and cardamom butter

You need to use really ripe mangoes for this recipe. If the mangoes are not ripe enough, they will need much longer cooking and will not produce such a richly flavoured butter.

Makes about 675g/1½lb

INGREDIENTS

900g/2lb ripe mangoes, peeled

6 green cardamom pods, split

120ml/4fl oz/½ cup freshly squeezed lemon juice

120ml/4fl oz/½ cup freshly squeezed orange juice

50ml/2fl oz/¼ cup water

675g/1½lb/scant 3½ cups granulated sugar, warmed

1 Cut the mango flesh away from the stones and chop, then place it in a pan with the cardamom pods, fruit juices and water.

2 Cover and simmer for 10 minutes. Remove the lid and simmer for a further 25 minutes, or until the mangoes are very soft and there is very little liquid left in the pan.

3 Remove the cardamom pods from the pan and discard. Transfer the fruit to a food processor and blend to a purée. Press the purée through a fine sieve into a bowl.

4 Measure the purée into a large, heavy pan, adding 275g/10oz/ 1⅓ cups warmed sugar for every 600ml/1 pint/2½ cups purée. Gently heat, stirring, until the sugar has dissolved. Increase the heat and boil for 10–20 minutes, stirring, until a thick butter forms that holds its shape when spooned on to a cold plate.

5 Spoon the mango and cardamom butter into small, warmed sterilized jars. Seal and label, then store in a cool, dark place for at least 2 days before eating. (The butter can be stored for up to 3 months.)

damson and vanilla cheese

You can use any type or variety of plum for this cheese, but damsons have the most intense flavour. This cheese is good with roast lamb, duck and game, or semi-soft cheese.

Makes about 900g/2lb

INGREDIENTS

1.5kg/3lb 6oz damsons
1 vanilla pod (bean), split
800g/1¾lb/4 cups granulated
   sugar, warmed

COOK'S TIPS

• When the cheese is ready, you should be able to see the base of the pan when a wooden spoon is drawn through the mixture. To test the set, spoon a small amount of the damson mixture on to a chilled plate; it should form a firm jelly.

• To make cheese shapes, spoon the mixture into greased moulds, and leave to set before turning out and serving.

1 Wash the damsons and place in a large pan with the vanilla pod and pour in enough water to come halfway up the fruit. Cover and simmer for 30 minutes.

2 Remove the vanilla pod from the pan and scrape the seeds back into the pan using the point of a knife.

3 Press the fruit and juices through a sieve into a bowl. Measure the purée into a large, heavy pan, adding 400g/14oz/ 2 cups sugar for every 600ml/ 1 pint/2½ cups purée.

4 Gently heat the purée, stirring, until the sugar has dissolved. Increase the heat slightly and cook for about 45 minutes, stirring frequently with a wooden spoon, until very thick.

5 Spoon the damson cheese into warmed, sterilized jars. Seal and label, then store in a cool, dark place for 2–3 months to dry out slightly before eating.

quince cheese

This wonderfully fragrant fruit cheese is particularly good set in squares, dusted with sugar and served as a sweetmeat, but it is just as good bottled in jars and spooned out as required.

Makes about 900g/2lb

INGREDIENTS

1.3kg/3lb quinces
800g/1¾lb/4 cups granulated
   sugar, warmed
caster (superfine) sugar, for dusting

COOK'S TIP

Rather than setting the cheese and cutting it into squares, simply spoon the mixture into warmed, sterilized, straight-sided jars. Seal and label, then store in a cool, dark place for 2–3 months to dry out slightly before eating.

1 Wash the quinces, then chop and place in a large pan. Pour in enough water to nearly cover the fruit, then cover with a lid and simmer for 45 minutes, or until the fruit is very tender. Cool slightly.

2 Press the mixture through a fine sieve into a bowl. Measure the purée into a large, heavy pan, adding 400g/14oz/2 cups sugar for every 600ml/1 pint/2½ cups purée. Heat gently, stirring, until the sugar has dissolved. Increase the heat and cook for 40–50 minutes, stirring frequently, until very thick (see Cook's Tip, left).

3 Pour the mixture into a small oiled baking tin (pan) and leave to set for 24 hours. Cut into small squares, dust with sugar and store in an airtight container.

spiced cherry cheese

For the best results, try to use cherries that have a good tart flavour and dark red flesh. Serve as an accompaniment to strong cheese, or sliced with roast duck or pork.

Makes about 900g/2lb

INGREDIENTS

1.5kg/3lb 6oz/8¼ cups cherries, stoned (pitted)

2 cinnamon sticks

800g/1¾lb/4 cups granulated sugar, warmed

COOK'S TIPS

• Store the cheese in a cool, dark place for 2–3 months before eating.

• To serve a fruit cheese in slices, turn it out of its container and slice using a sharp knife. The slices may be cut into smaller portions. Try to use a straight-sided container so that the cheese can slide out easily.

1 Place the cherries in a large pan with the cinnamon sticks. Pour in enough water to almost cover the fruit. Bring to the boil, then cover and simmer for 20–30 minutes, or until the cherries are very tender. Remove the cinnamon sticks from the pan and discard.

2 Tip the fruit into a sieve and press into a bowl, using the back of a spoon. Measure the purée into a large, heavy pan, adding 350g/12oz/1¾ cups warmed sugar for every 600ml/1 pint/2½ cups purée.

3 Gently heat the purée, stirring, until the sugar dissolves. Increase the heat and cook for 45 minutes, stirring frequently, until very thick. To test, spoon a little of the cheese on to a cold plate; it should form a firm jelly.

4 Spoon into warmed, sterilized jars or oiled moulds. Seal, label, and store in a cool, dark place.

blackberry and apple cheese

This rich, dark preserve has an incredibly intense flavour and fabulous colour. For a fragrant twist, add a few raspberries – or even strawberries – in place of some of the blackberries.

Makes about 900g/2lb

INGREDIENTS

900g/2lb/8 cups blackberries

450g/1lb tart cooking apples, cut into chunks, with skins and cores intact

grated rind and juice of 1 lemon

800g/1¾lb/4 cups granulated sugar, warmed

1 Put the blackberries, apples and lemon rind and juice in a pan and pour in enough water to come halfway up the fruit. Bring to the boil, then uncover and simmer for 15–20 minutes or until the fruit is very soft.

2 Leave the fruit to cool slightly, then tip the mixture into a sieve and press into a bowl, using the back of a spoon. Measure the purée into a large, heavy pan, adding 400g/14oz/2 cups warmed sugar for every 600ml/1 pint/ 2½ cups purée.

3 Gently heat the purée, stirring, until the sugar dissolves. Increase the heat slightly and cook for 40–50 minutes, stirring frequently, until very thick (see Cook's Tip).

4 Spoon the blackberry and apple cheese into warmed, sterilized straight-sided jars or oiled moulds. Seal and label the jars or moulds, then store in a cool, dark place for 2–3 months to dry out slightly.

COOK'S TIP

When the cheese is ready, you should be able to see the base of the pan when a wooden spoon is drawn through the mixture. Spoon a small amount of the mixture on to a chilled plate; it should form a firm jelly.

sweet fruit preserves

Seasonal fruits bottled in spirits or syrups look stunning stacked in your store cupboard and taste divine spooned over ice cream, cakes and desserts. Some fruits can even be enjoyed on their own with just a spoonful of cream. Preserving in syrups and alcohol helps to retain the colour, texture and flavour of the fruit, while ensuring that it does not ferment or spoil on keeping. Alcohol also adds extra flavour and body and can turn simple preserved fruits into an indulgent treat.

mulled pears

These pretty pears in a warming spiced syrup make a tempting dessert, particularly during the cold winter months. Serve them with crème fraîche or vanilla ice cream, or in open tarts.

Makes about 1.3kg/3lb

INGREDIENTS

1.8kg/4lb small firm pears

1 orange

1 lemon

2 cinnamon sticks, halved

12 whole cloves

5cm/2in piece fresh root ginger, peeled and sliced

300g/11oz/1½ cups granulated sugar

1 bottle fruity light red wine

COOK'S TIP

Pears have a delicate flavour, so use a light, fruity wine such as Beaujolais or Merlot to make the syrup.

1 Peel the pears leaving the stalks intact. Peel very thin strips of rind from the orange and lemon, using a vegetable peeler. Pack the pears and citrus rind into large sterilized preserving jars, dividing the spices evenly between the jars.

2 Preheat the oven to 120°C/250°F/Gas ½. Put the sugar and wine in a large pan and heat gently, stirring, until the sugar has completely dissolved. Bring the mixture to the boil, then cook for 5 minutes.

3 Pour the wine syrup over the pears, making sure that there are no air pockets and that the fruits are completely covered with the syrup.

4 Cover the jars with their lids, but do not seal. Place them in the oven and cook for 2½–3 hours.

5 Carefully remove the jars from the oven, place on a dry dishtowel and seal. Leave the jars to cool completely, then label and store in a cool, dark place.

COOK'S TIP

To check that jars are properly sealed, leave them to cool for 24 hours, then loosen the clasp. Very carefully, try lifting the jar by the lid alone: if the jar is sealed properly, the lid should be fixed firmly enough to take the weight of the pot. Replace the clasp and store until ready to use.

poached spiced plums in brandy

Bottling plums in a spicy syrup is a great way to preserve the flavours of autumn and provide a store of instant desserts during the winter months. Serve them with whipped cream.

Makes about 900g/2lb

INGREDIENTS

600ml/1 pint/2½ cups brandy

rind of 1 lemon, peeled in a long strip

350g/12oz/1¾ cups caster (superfine) sugar

1 cinnamon stick

900g/2lb plums

VARIATION

Any member of the plum family can be preserved using this recipe. Try bottling damsons or wild yellow plums as a delicious alternative. Cherries will also work very well.

1 Put the brandy, lemon rind, sugar and cinnamon in a large pan and heat gently until the sugar dissolves. Add the plums and poach for 15 minutes until soft. Remove the fruit and pack in sterilized jars.

2 Boil the syrup rapidly until reduced by a third, then strain over the plums to cover. Seal the jars tightly. Label when cold and store for up to 6 months in a cool, dark place.

apricots in amaretto syrup

Amaretto brings out the delicious flavour of apricots. Try serving the drained fruit on top of a tart filled with crème pâtissière, using some of the amaretto syrup to glaze the apricots.

2 Add the apricots to the syrup and bring almost to the boil. Cover and simmer gently for 5 minutes. Remove the apricots with a slotted spoon and drain in a colander.

3 Add the remaining sugar to the pan and heat gently, stirring until the sugar has dissolved, then boil rapidly until the syrup reaches 104°C/219°F. Cool slightly, then remove the vanilla pod and stir in the amaretto.

4 Pack the apricots loosely in large, warmed sterilized jars. Pour the syrup over, twisting and tapping the jars to expel any air. Seal and store in a cool, dark place for 2 weeks before eating.

Makes about 900g/2lb

INGREDIENTS

1.3kg/3lb firm apricots
1 litre/1¾ pints/4 cups water
800g/1¾lb/4 cups granulated sugar
1 vanilla pod (bean)
175ml/6fl oz/¾ cup amaretto liqueur

COOK'S TIP

For the best results, make this preserve when apricots are in season. Choose firm, unblemished fruits blushed with pink, that give slightly when squeezed gently in the palm of the hand.

1 Cut a slit in each apricot and remove the stone (pit), keeping the fruit intact. Put the water, half the sugar and the vanilla pod in a large pan, heat gently, stirring, until the sugar dissolves. Increase the heat and simmer for 5 minutes.

figs infused with earl grey

The aromatic Earl Grey tea in this syrup permeates the figs to create a sweet and intriguing flavour. They are delicious spooned over creamy Greek yogurt.

Makes about 1.8kg/4lb

INGREDIENTS

900g/2lb ready-to-eat dried figs
1.2 litres/2 pints/5 cups Earl Grey tea
pared rind of 1 orange
1 cinnamon stick
275g/10oz/1⅓ cups granulated sugar
250ml/8fl oz/1 cup brandy

VARIATION

Use Grand Marnier or Cointreau instead of brandy to emphasize the flavour of zesty orange in the syrup.

1 Put the figs in a pan and add the tea, orange rind and cinnamon stick. Bring to the boil, cover and simmer for 10–15 minutes, or until the figs are tender.

2 Using a slotted spoon, remove the figs from the pan and leave to drain. Add the sugar to the tea and heat gently, stirring, until the sugar has dissolved. Boil rapidly for 2 minutes until syrupy.

3 Remove the pan from the heat, then stir in the brandy. Pack the figs and orange rind into warmed sterilized jars and pour in the hot syrup to cover. Twist and gently tap the jars to expel any air bubbles, then seal and store in a cool, dark place for 1 month.

peaches in peach schnapps

The fragrant taste of peaches is complemented and intensified by the addition of the schnapps. Serve with whipped cream flavoured with some of the syrup and a squeeze of lemon juice.

Makes about 1.3kg/3lb

INGREDIENTS

1.3kg/3lb firm peaches

1 litre/1¾ pints/4 cups water

900g/2lb/4½ cups granulated sugar

8 green cardamom pods

50g/2oz/½ cup whole blanched almonds, toasted

120ml/4fl oz/½ cup peach schnapps

VARIATION

Amaretto, an Italian liqueur flavoured with almond and apricot kernels, can be used instead of peach schnapps.

1 Put the peaches in a bowl and pour over boiling water. Drain immediately and peel, then halve and remove the stones (pits).

2 Put the water and half the sugar in a large pan and heat gently until the sugar has dissolved. Increase the heat and boil for 5 minutes.

3 Add the peaches to the syrup and return to the boil. Reduce the heat, cover and simmer gently for 5–10 minutes, or until tender but not too soft. Using a slotted spoon, remove the peaches and set aside to drain.

4 Put the cardamom pods and almonds in a large pan, then add 900ml/1½ pints/3¾ cups of the syrup and the remaining sugar.

5 Gently heat the syrup, stirring until the sugar has dissolved. Bring to the boil and boil until the syrup reaches 104°C/219°F. Leave to cool slightly, remove the cardamom pods, then stir in the schnapps.

6 Pack the peaches loosely in warmed sterilized jars. Pour the syrup and almonds over the fruit, twisting and gently tapping the jars to release any air bubbles. Seal and store in a cool, dark place for 2 weeks before eating.

pineapple in coconut rum

The tropical flavour of pineapple is enhanced by the addition of coconut rum. For a really special treat, serve topped with whipped cream and grated bitter chocolate.

3 Add the remaining sugar to the syrup and heat, stirring, until the sugar has dissolved completely. Bring to the boil and boil for about 10 minutes, or until the syrup has thickened. Remove from the heat and set aside to cool slightly, then stir in the coconut rum.

4 Pack the drained pineapple loosely in warmed sterilized jars. Pour in the syrup until the fruit is covered, tapping and twisting the jars to release any air bubbles. Seal, label and store in a cool, dark place for 2 weeks before eating.

COOK'S TIP

Choose plump pineapples that feel heavy for their size, with fresh, stiff plumes. To test for ripeness, gently pull out one of the bottom leaves; it should come out easily.

Makes about 900g/2lb

INGREDIENTS

1 orange

1.2 litres/2 pints/5 cups water

900g/2lb/4½ cups granulated sugar

2 pineapples, peeled, cored and cut into small chunks

300ml/½ pint/1¼ cups coconut rum

1 Thinly pare strips of rind from the orange, then slice into thin matchsticks. Put the water and half the sugar in a large pan with the orange rind and heat gently until the sugar has dissolved. Increase the heat and boil for 5 minutes.

2 Carefully add the pineapple pieces to the syrup and return to the boil. Reduce the heat and simmer gently for 10 minutes. Using a slotted spoon, remove the pineapple from the pan and set aside to drain.

clementines in juniper syrup

Whole clementines preserved in spiced syrup make a lovely dessert served on their own, with just a spoonful of mascarpone or clotted cream. They also make an excellent addition to trifles.

Makes about 1.3kg/3lb

INGREDIENTS

5cm/2in piece fresh root ginger, sliced

6 whole cloves, plus extra for the jars

5ml/1 tsp juniper berries, crushed, plus extra for the jars

900g/2lb/4½ cups granulated sugar

1.2 litres/2 pints/5 cups water

1.3kg/3lb clementines, peeled

COOK'S TIPS

• These pretty spiced clementines look fabulous packed in attractive jars and make an excellent Christmas gift for friends and family.

• When peeling the clementines, try to remove as much of the white pith from the fruit as possible.

1 Tie the ginger, cloves and juniper berries together in a small muslin (cheesecloth) bag.

2 Put the sugar and water in a large pan and heat gently, stirring, until the sugar has dissolved. Add the spice bag to the pan, bring to the boil and cook for 5 minutes.

3 Add the clementines to the pan and simmer for 8–10 minutes, or until tender. Using a slotted spoon, remove the fruit from the syrup and drain well.

4 Pack the hot fruit into warmed sterilized jars and add a few cloves and juniper berries to each jar. Pour off any excess liquid.

5 Return the syrup to the boil and boil rapidly for 10 minutes. Leave the syrup to cool slightly, then pour over the fruit to cover completely. Twist and gently tap the jars to release any trapped air bubbles, then seal and store in a cool, dark place.

kumquats and limequats in brandy syrup

These yellow and green fruits are highly decorative and taste very good indeed, so make a few extra jars of this luxurious preserve to enjoy throughout the coming months. For a really indulgent dessert, serve with good-quality chocolate ice cream or a creamy baked custard.

Makes about 900g/2lb

INGREDIENTS

450g/1lb kumquats and limequats

175g/6oz/scant 1 cup granulated sugar

600ml/1 pint/2½ cups water

150ml/¼ pint/⅔ cup brandy

15ml/1 tbsp orange flower water

COOK'S TIP

Kumquats and limequats are unusual among the citrus family because they are eaten whole and do not need to be peeled. Their thin skins have a pleasantly bitter flavour.

1 Using a cocktail stick (toothpick), prick each individual kumquat and limequat several times.

2 Put the sugar and water in a large pan and heat, stirring, until the sugar has dissolved. Bring to the boil, add the fruit and simmer for 25 minutes, or until tender. Using a slotted spoon, remove the fruit to warmed, sterilized jars.

3 The syrup should be fairly thick: if not, boil for a few minutes, then leave to cool very slightly.

4 Stir the brandy and orange flower water into the syrup, then pour over the fruit and seal immediately. Store in a cool, dark place and use within 6 months.

forest berries in kirsch

This preserve captures the essence of the season in its rich, dark colour and flavour. Adding the sweet cherry liqueur Kirsch to the syrup intensifies the flavour of the bottled fruit.

Makes about 1.3kg/3lb

INGREDIENTS

1.3kg/3lb/12 cups mixed prepared summer berries, such as blackberries, raspberries, strawberries, redcurrants and cherries

225g/8oz/generous 1 cup granulated sugar

600ml/1 pint/2½ cups water

120ml/4fl oz/½ cup Kirsch

COOK'S TIP

Be careful not to overcook the fruits because they will lose their beautiful colour and fresh flavour.

1 Preheat the oven to 120°C/ 250°F/Gas ½. Pack the prepared fruit loosely into sterilized jars. Cover without sealing and place in the oven for 50–60 minutes, or until the juices start to run.

2 Meanwhile, put the sugar and water in a large pan and heat gently, stirring, until the sugar has dissolved. Increase the heat, bring to the boil and boil for 5 minutes. Stir in the Kirsch and set aside.

3 Carefully remove the jars from the oven and place on a dishtowel. Use the fruit from one of the jars to top up the rest.

4 Pour the boiling syrup into each jar, twisting and tapping each one to ensure that no air bubbles have been trapped. Seal, then store in a cool, dark place.

cherries in eau de vie

These potent cherries should be consumed with respect as they pack quite an alcoholic punch. Serve them with rich, dark chocolate torte or as a wicked topping for creamy rice pudding.

2 Spoon the sugar over the fruit, then pour in the eau de vie to cover and seal tightly.

3 Store for at least 1 month before serving, shaking the bottle now and then to help dissolve the sugar.

COOK'S TIP

Eau de vie actually refers to all spirits distilled from fermented fruits. Eau de vie is always colourless, with a high alcohol content (sometimes 45% ABV) and a clean, pure scent and the flavour of the founding fruit. Popular eaux de vie are made from cherries and strawberries.

Makes about 1.3kg/3lb

INGREDIENTS

450g/1lb/generous 3 cups ripe cherries
8 blanched almonds
75g/3oz/6 tbsp granulated sugar
500ml/17fl oz/scant 2¼ cups eau de vie

VARIATIONS

Strawberries, raspberries and blackcurrants are all excellent preserved in eau de vie. They will all produce fine fruity liqueurs as well as the macerated fruit.

1 Wash and stone (pit) the cherries then pack them into a sterilized, wide-necked bottle along with the blanched almonds.

blackcurrant brandy

Spoon a little of the brandy into a wine glass and top up with chilled white wine or champagne for a special celebration drink. Alternatively serve in small liqueur glasses as a digestif.

Makes about 1 litre/1¾ pints/4 cups

INGREDIENTS

900g/2lb/8 cups blackcurrants, washed
600ml/1 pint/2½ cups brandy
350g/12oz/1¾ cups granulated sugar

COOK'S TIP

When you have strained off the brandy, reserve the blackcurrants and freeze for later use. They are great added to fruit salads and trifles, or make a delicious richly flavoured ice cream topping. Be careful though, because they pack quite a boozy punch.

1 Strip the blackcurrants off their stems and pack the fruit into a sterilized 1.5 litre/2½ pint/6¼ cup preserving jar. Using the back of a wooden spoon, crush the blackcurrants lightly.

2 Add the brandy and sugar to the jar, ensuring the fruit is completely covered by the brandy. Twist and gently tap the jar to ensure there are no trapped air bubbles.

3 Seal the jar, then store in a cool, dark place for about 2 months, shaking the jar occasionally.

4 Pour the liquor through a sieve lined with a double layer of muslin (cheesecloth) into a sterilized jug (pitcher). Pour into sterilized bottles, seal, label and store in a cool, dark place.

blueberries in gin syrup

These aromatic berries preserved in a gin-laced syrup make a wonderful topping for vanilla ice cream. The syrup turns a fabulous blue colour and the distinctive flavour of the gin complements, rather than masks, the essence of the blueberries.

Makes about 1.8kg/4lb

INGREDIENTS

1.3kg/3lb/12 cups blueberries
225g/8oz/1 cup granulated sugar
600ml/1 pint/2½ cups water
120ml/4fl oz/½ cup gin

1 Preheat the oven to 120°C/ 250°F/Gas ½. Pack the blueberries into sterilized jars and cover, without sealing. Put the jars in the oven and bake for 50–60 minutes until the juices start to run.

2 Meanwhile, put the sugar and water in a pan and gently heat, stirring continuously, until the sugar has dissolved completely. Increase the heat and boil for 5 minutes. Stir in the gin.

3 Carefully remove the jars from the oven and place on a dry dishtowel. Use the fruit from one of the jars to top up the others.

4 Carefully pour the boiling gin syrup into the jars to completely cover the fruit. Twist and gently tap the jars to ensure that no air bubbles have been trapped.

5 Seal, then store in a cool, dark place until ready to serve.

rumtopf

This fruit preserve originated in Germany, where special earthenware rumtopf pots are traditionally filled with fruits as they come into season. It is not necessary to use the specific pot; you can use a large preserving jar instead. Store in a cool, dark place.

Makes about 3 litres/5 pints/12½ cups

INGREDIENTS

900g/2lb fruit, such as strawberries, blackberries, blackcurrants, redcurrants, peaches, apricots, cherries and plums

250g/9oz/1¼ cups granulated sugar

1 litre/1¾ pints/4 cups white rum

1 Prepare the fruit: remove stems, skins, cores and stones (pits) and cut larger fruit into bitesize pieces. Combine the fruit and sugar in a large non-metallic bowl, cover and leave to stand for 30 minutes.

2 Spoon the fruit and juices into a sterilized 3 litre/5 pint/12½ cup preserving or earthenware jar and pour in the white rum to cover.

3 Cover the jar with clear film (plastic wrap), then seal and store in a cool, dark place.

4 As space allows, and as different fruits come into season, add more fruit, sugar and rum in appropriate proportions, as described above.

5 When the jar is full, store in a cool, dark place for 2 months. Serve the fruit spooned over ice cream or other desserts and enjoy the rum in glasses as a liqueur.

spiced apple mincemeat

This fruity mincemeat is traditionally used to fill little pies at Christmas but it is great at any time. Try it as a filling for large tarts finished with a lattice top and served with custard. To make a lighter mincemeat, add some extra grated apple just before using.

Makes about 1.8kg/4lb

INGREDIENTS

500g/1¼lb tart cooking apples, peeled, cored and finely diced

115g/4oz/½ cup ready-to-eat dried apricots, coarsely chopped

900g/2lb/5⅓ cups luxury dried mixed fruit

115g/4oz/1 cup whole blanched almonds, chopped

175g/6oz/1 cup shredded beef or vegetarian suet (chilled, grated shortening)

225g/8oz/generous 1 cup dark muscovado (molasses) sugar

grated rind and juice of 1 orange

grated rind and juice of 1 lemon

5ml/1 tsp ground cinnamon

2.5ml/½ tsp grated nutmeg

2.5ml/½ tsp ground ginger

120ml/4fl oz/½ cup brandy

1 Put the apples, apricots, dried fruit, almonds, suet and sugar in a large non-metallic bowl and stir together until thoroughly combined.

2 Add the orange and lemon rind and juice, cinnamon, nutmeg, ginger and brandy and mix well. Cover the bowl with a clean dishtowel and leave to stand in a cool place for 2 days, stirring occasionally.

3 Spoon the mincemeat into cool sterilized jars, pressing down well, and being very careful not to trap any air bubbles. Cover and seal.

4 Store the jars in a cool, dark place for at least 4 weeks before using. Once opened, store in the refrigerator and use within 4 weeks. Unopened, the mincemeat will keep for 1 year.

COOK'S TIP

If, when opened, the mincemeat seems dry, pour a little extra brandy or orange juice into the jar and gently stir in. You may need to remove a spoonful or two of the mincemeat from the jar to do this.

INDEX